WRITTEN BY

MARCO ZAPPIA

smartest guy in the room

DEDICATION

The heavens opened up, and God sent me the most beautiful angel he ever created, my wife. Her halo is slightly crooked, and that's what contributes to her wonderful charm and feisty personality. For over fifty years, she walked two feet ahead of me kicking the pebbles out of the way so that I wouldn't trip. You're my life, sweetheart. Whatever I accomplished, I never could have done it without you. To you, my angel, I dedicate this book.

FORWARD

I was very fortunate to find a career that I really loved. Then to be able to team up with my beautiful and brilliant wife for twenty-five years was the icing on the cake. I hope that hearing my story in some way will help you understand what I think is the role of the editor.

The trouble with trying to write about what you've accomplished is that by the time you're ready to write about it, your memory is not what it used to be. I apologize to all of the great production people and crew members that I worked with in the past for not remembering your names. I do remember all of the great work we did together, and for that I thank you.

TABLE OF CONTENTS

CHAPTER ONE

The Journey Begins

A lot of books have been written on the subject of videotape editing, but they are mostly how-to books. Instead, I want to talk about the editors themselves and what roles they play in the whole process of creating a television show. I would also like to talk about the evolution of videotape editing. I think the best way to do that is to recount some of my own experiences from forty years in the industry.

I've often been asked which college I attended and what degree I had in order to get my first editing job, which was at CBS. People also ask who I knew, since "No one ever got into a network without a connection." To answer these questions, I'd like to start by telling you a little about myself.

My parents were Italian immigrants who came over from Italy through Ellis Island with their parents. They were married when they were twenty years old. My dad was a shoe cobbler who had a little shop with living quarters in the back. My parents were married for sixty years, and I was one of twelve kids—seven boys and five girls. My mom worked alongside my dad, whether he was repairing shoes, raising chickens on a ranch in Riverside California, or making carpet floor mats for all models of cars. We had the most wonderful parents you could ever hope to have. We never felt we were denied anything. They had to be angels to raise twelve kids the way they did, but that'll be another book.

When my wife, Carole Ann, and I got married, she was nineteen and I was twenty-three. I had opened a TV repair shop, and Carole Ann not only answered the phones (they rang through to our home), she also took care of kids for extra money. We couldn't afford any furniture except a couch that turned into a bed and an old black-and-white TV set. We didn't have a refrigerator or washing machine; so twice a week I brought home fifty pounds of ice and put it in the laundry tub to keep the food cold.

I loved working with my hands, so I repaired all small appliances as well as TV sets. There was only one problem: I was a lousy businessman. I charged $2.50 for a house call. I remember one time I went to a house with five small children. The joy on those kids' faces when I finally fixed the TV set was amazing. I replaced about $30 worth of parts, but when I presented the bill to the parents, they informed me that they didn't have the money to pay me. I didn't have the heart to unfix the TV to get my parts back. I told them they could pay me whenever they had the money. You didn't have to hit me over the head with a two-by-four: that's when I realized that working for myself was not a very good idea.

Consequently, I applied for and got a job at RCA as a TV repairman for seventy dollars a week. With the money my wife earned taking care of kids and my large (I thought) salary, we were in the money. I mostly worked in the Beverly Hills area. The color TV sets in those days went through quite an intensive set-up procedure when they were delivered to the house. So the closest I came to the broadcast industry in those days was when I went to the homes of Carol Burnett, Joey Bishop, Robert Goulet, Dean Martin, and many others to set up their TV sets.

Most people can tell you what they were doing when the thirty-fifth president of the United States, John F. Kennedy, was assassinated on November 22, 1963. I'll never forget that day. I was in Beverly Hills walking up the steps of an RCA TV customer's home to service his TV set. I rang the doorbell, and when the gentlemen came to the door, he said, "Quick, fix the TV set! The president of the United States and governor of Texas has been shot. I want to watch the news."

It didn't take very long to fix the set; afterward we just sat and watched the news. The network played the shooting of the president over and over. The whole country was in shock, and for the rest of the day not much work was done. The nation was in mourning for weeks after that.

Shortly afterwards, on November 29 1963, our daughter, Roxanne Marie, was born. It was an extra special day for my wife and me because November 29 is also my birthday as well as Carole Ann's, and now we share that day with our daughter.

I began attending night school at the Western Institute of Electronics to get a degree in electrical engineering because I believe in the following rule of life:

Always try to advance your education in whatever field interests you. The more knowledge you have, the more you'll be able to take advantage of any opportunities that come your way.

One day, Carole Ann told me about a job listing she saw in the newspaper for a maintenance engineer in the videotape department at CBS. I told her that I didn't know anything about the broadcast industry, and I knew I wasn't qualified for a job like that. Nonetheless, she encouraged me to go to apply anyway. She said, "Even if you don't get the job this time, when the opportunity comes up again, you could apply knowing a lot more about what the job requires." So kicking and screaming, I went to the library and checked out all the books I could on broadcast videotape machines. I memorized as much as I could about the equipment, hoping I could convince CBS I knew more than I did.

With my newfound knowledge, I went to CBS on my lunch hour and applied for the job. The interviewers gave me engineering and color blindness tests before they talked to me. To my surprise, by the time I got back to RCA, there was a phone call from my wife telling me that CBS wanted to hire me. That girl sure has good instincts

Maybe I should listen to her more often.

It was 1968, and I was the first person hired at CBS in twenty-five years. I found out that nobody left CBS until they retired. Of the three networks, if you wanted to learn anything about the broadcast industry, CBS was the best place to be. It had the best engineers, editors, camera operators, and production people. It also had the best retirement and stock option plans in the business.

After my two-week notice to RCA was up, I found myself standing in front of the CBS network building at Beverly and Fairfax, a three-story, black-and-white building with large glass doors at the entrance. At the top of the building, three large black letters stood out: **"CBS."** Boy, was that impressive—and a little intimidating. The building held four sound stages (studios 31, 33, 41, and 43), plus office space and technical facilities. (A renovation in the 1980s added two new sound stages—studios 36 and 46—and more office space and technical facilities such as editing rooms and storage.)

My career in the broadcasting industry was about to begin. I was a little nervous about what was in store for me. but there was no turning back at that point. So, I entered through the large glass doors of the building, and as I walked down the hallways, I couldn't help but notice that the walls were lined with poster-size pictures of all the stars that had done shows in this building. What a great lineup: Red Skeleton, Liza Minnelli, Dinah Shore, Danny Kaye, Doris Day, Jimmy Durante, and on and on.

I was to report to the videotape department, which was located in the basement. I went downstairs and found a beehive of activity. I could hear the loud hum of video-tape machines, and there must have been twenty people in the room running the machines, loading tapes, editing and working on the equipment. I felt a little apprehensive since I got the job by reading a couple of books, passing a written test or two, and relying on my ability to, well, em-bellish, exaggerate, or stretch the truth about what I really knew about the equipment.

I went to the large scheduling desk where Kelsey, one of the videotape supervisors, greeted me. He took me on the fifty-cent tour. He pointed out that there were sixteen Ampex videotape machines where the shows were re-corded from the East Coast and then played back to the West Coast three hours later. He said, "This is also the de-partment where all the news and show editing is done, and where they record the shows from the sound stages here at the complex." These were the years CBS had some of the best variety shows on the air—shows starring Carol Burnett, Red Skelton, Doris Day, Judy Garland, Danny Kaye, Liza Minnelli, Sonny and Cher, and many more.

Kelsey also took me to the engineering department. After the tour, Kelsey said, "We're going to start you in operations where the shows are recorded and played back for air. That way you can get a feel for how the department operates."

Dan E. Cain was assigned to train me. He showed me how they would record the feed from the East Coast as the shows were airing there. Dan told me that, "if the feed wasn't recorded properly, a special feed had to be scheduled to redo the recording, but at great expense." Three hours later the recorded shows were broadcast on the West Coast.

The Ampex 1000 was used for backup, and the Ampex 2000 was used for the air feed; these machines were set side by side. First we patched the machines to record the feed from the East Coast. Afterwards all the levels were set to broadcast standards, video, audio and color. The two tapes were then cued up in sync with each other with a five-second pre-roll. Control of the two machines was then re-routed to Program Control (PC) who, when the time came, started the machines and put the show or commercial on the air. This process was really quite an experience. I not only learned about the machines but also the operation of the whole department.

The tapes were two inches wide, and the reels came in thirty-, sixty- and ninety-minute loads. After a few days, I was on my own. I was recording and playing back shows like *Mannix*, *Gunsmoke*, the original *Hawaii Five-O*, and *Mission: Impossible*, to name a few. I couldn't believe that I actually got paid to watch these great shows.

After I was at CBS for a while, one of the operators loaded a ninety-minute reel on the playback side and a thirty-minute empty reel on the take-up side. He didn't realize until he was almost thirty minutes into the show that the take-up reel was too small, so the tape would soon spill over onto the floor. You can imagine how he reacted. I happened to be on the machines across from him when, in a panic, he sought help. I walked over to his machines to see what he had done and told him it was an easy fix and not to worry. The most important thing was to keep the show on the air. I hit the intercom and asked PC to switch over to the Ampex 1000 first chance they had because a problem was coming up with the air machine, and we needed a few minutes to fix it. The quality of the back up machine was poor, so they didn't like to use it except for emergencies.

Once PC switched over, we pulled an empty tall trashcan over to the air machine and placed it under the take-up reel, which was nearly full. While the tape was still running, I waited for a good spot to cut the tape as it kept playing so that it could neatly run into the trash can instead of overflowing onto the floor. When we saw that everything was running smoothly, I gave the machine back to PC, and when the show finished airing, we carefully rewound the tape back onto the playback side. I asked one of the editors if he could splice the tape back together where I had cut it, and we then finished rewinding the tape back onto the original reel.

There are times when a cool head and a little common sense go a long way.

Since I had an engineering degree, after three or four months I was assigned to the maintenance department. My shift was from four o'clock in the morning until noon. Jim Russell headed the department, but I worked with Paul Morrison and Roger Ellis the most. I did some preventative maintenance such as cleaning the video and audio heads, setting the timing, checking the number of hours of use on the video heads, and monitoring various technical readings.

When an operator called for maintenance, the routine was that four or five of us would go to the area and check on the problem. This situation gave me a chance to watch the maintenance guys in action and learn. All I knew about the tape machines was that the tape was two inches wide and the Ampex 1000 had two large racks of Raytheon tubes that threw off enough heat to keep me warm on any cold morning. However, I learned quickly, and, after a while, I was actually able to contribute to the repairs. I guess my work on TV sets and all types of electronic appliances and equipment both at Marco's TV VILLE and RCA had prepared me for the job at CBS more than I had thought. I was learning how to work on all the equipment, and I started to really like my job.

Never underestimate the value of some of your past experiences. They will always be there for you to call back on for use in future jobs.

One morning, Jim the editor and one of the news producers were editing a news piece. I was amazed at how the editing was done in those days. They used a Smith Editor that consisted of a microscope; a splicing block with a special bar, a very sharp razor, and a special solution loaded with alcohol and powdered iron shavings.

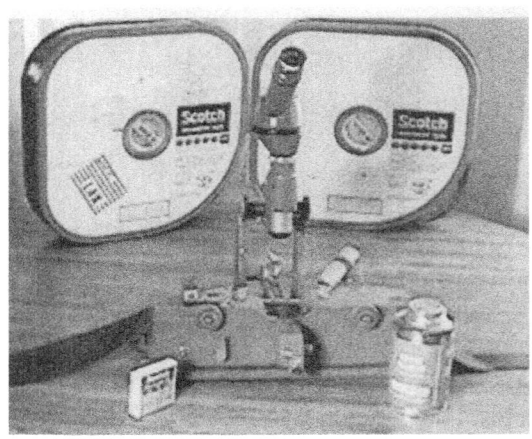

Smith splicer with two inch video tape

At that time these machines had neither slow motion nor freeze-frame capabilities. Therefore, the editor had to find the edit point (where you want the output of one clip to meet the input of the next clip) by playing the tape and by knowing how the tape moved through the machine. He was able to get very close to the edit point that way. The fact that the sound was laid down fifteen frames ahead of the corresponding

Picture meant that simple level sync cuts were impossible. Sound had to be copied off to a one-fourth-inch audictape and then lay back onto the two-inch edit tape.

After the editor found his outgoing edit point, he marked the tape on the outside with a marking pen. The tape was then played to where he wanted to come back in and marked at that point. After cutting the tape at each marking point, he put the first section of tape on the editing block and applied a strip of the solution to the tape where he wanted to make the splice. The tape was placed under the microscope where he could see narrow rows of iron particles that showed the video field below each control track.

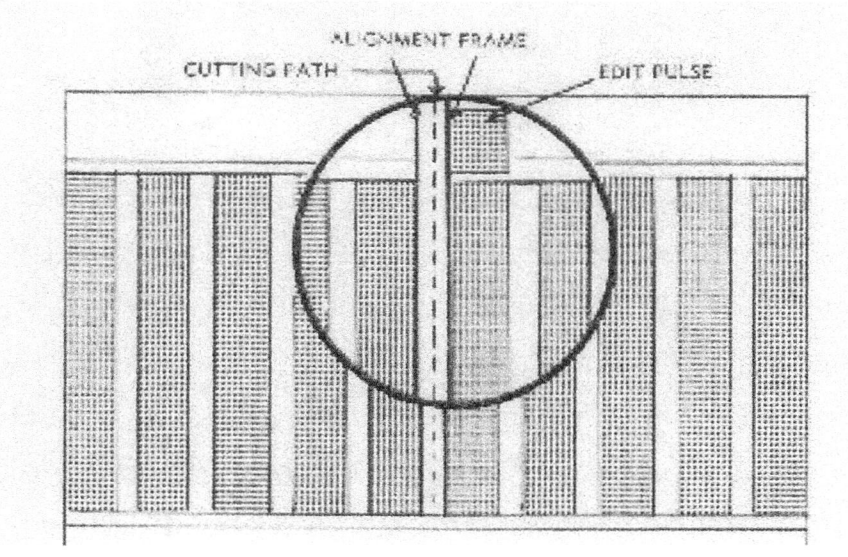

This is what was seen through the microscope

The editor cut between the video fields, and the second piece of tape was prepared in the same manner. Both pieces were taped together with a piece of Mylar tape.

13

The end result was an edit that he hoped would play well through the video heads.

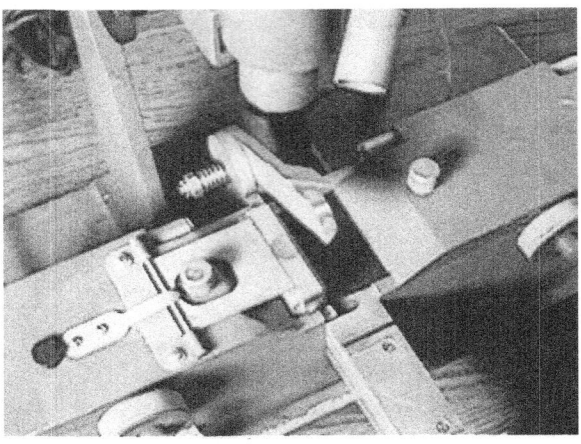

Splicing block portion of the Smith Editor

Sometimes when the splice passed through, the upper portion of the screen jarred to one side for a few frames after the edit point. Other times you'd see a brief flash of snow after the edit point and, every once in a while, the tape would come apart, and the machine would come to a stop. There were those rare occasions, though, when the splice would go through without disrupting the image and you would have a perfect edit.

As I was watching the news piece being edited, I heard the producer trying to tell Jim, the editor, what he wanted. Jim didn't seem to understand. I called him aside and told him that I thought the producer wanted him to cut out the middle of the sentence and bridge the cut with a couple of shots of the crowd. I wasn't quite sure if this could even be done or how he would do it, but Jim thanked me, and I went back to my repairs.

Later that day the operations supervisor, Kelsey, called me over and asked me why I hadn't told him that I knew about editing. I told him that I didn't know anything about editing and asked where he got the idea that I did. He said that Jim had told him what had happened that morning and explained that the solution I suggested was a technique of editing. I then said, "Kelsey, I could tell him what I thought the producer wanted him to do, but I certainly couldn't do it." Kelsey said he needed me back in operations to help the editors, because he knew that I could easily learn the physical aspects of editing.

As always when I needed to whine to somebody about a problem, I went home and talked to my wife about it. I told her the situation and that I was a hands-on technician, not an editor. Once again she was the voice of reason. She said, "If that's what they want you to do, you should try it out for six months. If it doesn't work out, you can always go back to maintenance. But who knows? Maybe you will end up liking it."

"That won't happen," I said, but I knew she was right.

The lesson here is that sometimes your wife really does know what's best. I hate when that happens.

When I went back to work the next day, my boss Charlie told me that they were sending five or six people from the videotape department to the Democratic National Convention in Chicago, and he wanted me to go with the editors. My wife was pregnant with our son, and she was expecting any day. She said, "Don't worry. I'll be fine. If anything happens, my mom will be here." Reluctantly, I went. Early the next morning, I drove to the airport and hopped on a plane for Chicago. I had mixed feelings about going. This was my first trip outside of California, and the first time on a plane.

It was also the first time away from my wife in seven years of our marriage. However, it was a good opportunity to learn more about working on events outside the studios. When the plane landed, we drove to our hotel. We were booked at a Holiday Inn near the lake. The room wasn't very nice, but it didn't matter because, after that first night we wouldn't be seeing our room for two weeks.

The next morning at 6:00 a.m., we drove to the Chicago Hilton Hotel at the corner of Michigan Avenue and Balboa

Street where the convention was to be held. Our remote trucks were parked in front of the hotel where we would be working. It was the last week in August, and even though it was warm and sunny when I left California, Chicago was cold and windy. Since I was a native Californian, I had never felt that kind of cold.

The 1968 Chicago National Convention marked the height of the '60s protest movement. The Vietnam War divided the country, and in that year both Robert F. Kennedy and Dr. Martin Luther King, Jr. had been assassinated. Demonstrators and police had been clashing in the streets of Chicago for over a week by the time we arrived.

One of the best editors at CBS, Bill Kendall, and I stayed in the truck for twenty-four hours a day. Our job was to record and edit any action from the demonstrators. If we had anything interesting, we'd play it back during the convention when they needed it. We took turns sleeping on the floor of the truck when we could.

One evening Bill and I were editing a news piece to be played during the convention the next day. We were watching the footage, and the producer told me to start the piece at the point where the policemen were beating on the demonstrators. I asked him, "Don't you want to start where the demonstrators were throwing rocks, glass, and anything they could get their hands on?" He said, "Start the tapes where I asked you to start." I persisted: "Isn't that a little one-sided?"

Needless to say, the next day I was assigned to the trucks near Grant Park. I was used as an audio utility man. One day as the riots in the park started up again, one of the news producers handed me a mike and said, "We aren't getting any audio. Run into the middle of the crowd and hold up the mike." Now I have to admit, in those days I wasn't the sharpest pencil in the drawer because I took the mike and ran into the crowd. The people were really worked up. I was being crushed, pulled, and pushed as they were trying to take the mike away from me. Before I got trampled, the police pulled me out of the middle of the angry crowd. I guess the audio I got while I was being attacked was good enough because that's what the producers used.

Once the convention was finally over, we went back to our hotels. I took a much-needed shower and packed my bags for the airport. Boy, was I glad when we landed in good old, sunny California. Leaving California was quite an experience, but I thought once was enough—never again. My wife still hadn't delivered our baby. I guess they wanted to wait for me to get back, so on September 10, 1968, our son Robert Michael was born.

When I got back to work, CBS was installing a new electronic editing system. My boss said he wanted me to help finish the installation then learn as much as I could about the operation of the system so that I could train the editors to use it. We were installing the EECO-900 EDITOR, a new and innovative system that enabled editing to be done between two machines using time code recorded on one of the audio tracks on the videotapes. With this system the editor had greater control and flexibility over the editing process.

The way the EECO-900 worked was that the recorded material was loaded on the playback machine, and the time code numbers were dialed in from the script page you wanted the tape to cue to. As a result, the tape automatically cued to the number dialed. By playing the tape and stopping where you wanted the edit to start, you were able to mark the tape on the outside with a sharpie. Then a tape with black video with the time code recorded on it—essentially a, "blank canvas" for the editor—was placed on the record machine. You dialed in the numbered section, overlaid it on the black video, and started to build the master. This way you could preview the edit to see how close you were. Pretty soon you could judge how much to move the playback tape forward or backward to allow for a frame. Sometimes you had several marks on the tape before you found the edit point.

During the 1960s and the 1970s, CBS had some of the best editors in the business. To name a few, there were Jim Bracy, Bill Kendall, Jean De Craig, Jay Cook and Lew Smith. These guys could make edits between words or musical notes with great accuracy using a razor blade. All I had to do once we had the EECO-900 was to convince them to give up the hands-on-razor editing for electronic editing.

One of the concerns of our CBS editors was that they could make the edits so fast with this system that they would lose all their overtime—or even some jobs. But I explained to them that would never happen because the directors would quickly realize that they could be more creative once more complicated edits were possible. I said, "You'll be able to make edits that couldn't be done before, either because making the physical splice took too long, or what the director wanted wasn't possible with the old equpment. With this machine, more is possible, so you'll be working longer hours. In addition, jobs will be created because each editor will need an assistant to load and cue up the tapes on the playback machine." They agreed to try it only if I assisted each of them until they learned the system. I told them that I would, and the training began.

After a week of training, one of their complaints was that they thought electronic editing was less creative because they missed that feeling of holding the tape in their hands and cutting it. They felt they had more control over the edit when they could feel the tape. That was something I didn't understand at that time. Soon they begin to appreciate the fact that previewing the edit and adjusting the playback or record tapes a frame at a time, before they committed to the edit, would allow them to be more accurate. The editors were finally realizing that electronic editing was a tool that would make the physical aspects of editing much easier and would allow them to concentrate more on the creative side of editing. *Still, I could understand the editors' initial reluctance to change. These guys were at the top of their field, yet they were asked to change to a whole new way of editing.*

For the next three years, I assisted all the editors. It turned out to be a great learning experience for me as well as for them. While I was teaching them how to use the equipment, I was learning what editing was really about and what a creative process it was. Each editor had his own way of doing things, and I learned the best methods from each of them. Whenever I assisted, I tried to learn as much about the equipment as I could. I also wanted to learn what I needed to know to make it easier for the editors. That way I was able to anticipate what they wanted and keep one step ahead of them.

By trying to anticipate the editor's needs, you learn a lot more about editing as well as about the equipment. Plus, it's what a good assistant does.

The director sat with us at the machines and, as we played the tapes, he would tell us what he wanted. I was surprised how well I understood him. Before he finished his sentence, I had the playback machine cued up and ready. I noticed that sometimes the editor didn't quite understand what the director wanted. I think that was because the editor was too wrapped up in the technology, so he wasn't really listening to the director. I would quietly go to the editor and tell him that my machine was cued up to what I thought the director wanted, and I would then explain what I thought that was.

An example of this situation occurred when I was working on a Hallmark Hall of Fame movie called *The First Woman President*. The director was Delbert Mann, one of the top film directors, who in 1956 won an Oscar for the movie *Marty*. We started editing, but when Delbert told the editor what he wanted, there were times when the editor didn't understand, so I would explain it to him. When Delbert realized what was happening, he would tell both of us what he wanted. Then, when the editor didn't understand, I would quietly explain it to him. When we finished editing the movie, the director said to me, "If I knew how much you would be contributing to the editing process, I would have insisted that your name be listed on the credits as one of the editors." I thanked him, and I told him that working with him was a great learning experience, and that was enough for me.

This is a good time for me to recommend that video editors should learn the editing system so well that the operation is second nature to you. The edit system is something you should never have to think about.

CHAPTER TWO

———

MOVING UP WITH FAST CHANGING TECHNOLOGY

I n 1971 I was assisting Lew Smith on building a pre-Rose Parade half-hour show. It was all about how the floats were built as well as a little history of the parade itself. We had two days to finish the editing. We worked twenty-four hours straight and finished it with one day to spare. There was a lot of material to go through, and we made a lot of edits. For some reason, I got the idea to start making a paper edit list by writing down the edit time code numbers of each edit, in case we had to repair or change something in the show. Furthermore, I decided to make such a list for all the shows from then on.

When we were finished, I dragged myself home but, as soon as my head hit the pillow, the telephone rang. My wife said it was CBS. They told her that somebody in the tape vaults accidentally degaussed the master (the master tape was accidentally erased) that we had just built, so Lew and I had to go back in. We had less than twenty-four hours to re-edit the whole show. I wasn't too happy about going back in, but I knew that accidents like this happen and, with my edit list, we would get it done in time.

When I got in to work, Lew was already there. I told him about my paper edit list and, boy, was he relieved. We re-built the show in about five hours. We weren't taking any chances, so this time we waited around until a copy of the show was made before we left. About a week later, we got a nice letter from one of the CBS West Coast executives thanking us for what we did on the show.

1/10/72

TO: Marco Zappia

I am very grateful for the work that you did with Lew Smith in reediting the Tournament of Roses preshow in time for the Friday night viewing.

We were in a predicament and Lew and yourself bailed us out.

Again, thank you very much.

Bill Copeland

cc: Mr. Hesen

A lot of these stories I'm telling you will probably never happen to you. Technology today is so different, but the point is to try to anticipate what might lie ahead. Whether you're assisting or editing, such anticipation may just be a lifesaver.

I was working from sixty to eighty hours a week. Thank God I had a wonderful, understanding wife. She knew that I was working in a field that I really loved, so she took over everything else. All I had to do was edit.

At CBS we edited several variety shows: *The Danny Kaye Show*, *The Red Skelton Show*, *The Carol Burnett Show*, *The Doris Day Hour*, *The Glen Campbell Good Time Hour*, and *The Smothers Brothers*, among others. We did dramas, Hallmark Hall of Fame movies, and *Playhouse 90*. Once in a while, my boss would move me over to the editing chair for game shows, syndicated shows, *Insight* (a religious drama), or *Hour of Power*.

When I was editing one of the episodes of *Insight*, Father Kaiser, the executive producer, came in one afternoon to edit one of the scenes and view the whole show. I had reservations at a restaurant to take my wife out to dinner for our anniversary that night, and it was getting close to the time I needed to leave. After we finished viewing the whole show, Father Kaiser wanted to do some fixes. I turned to him and asked, "Father, do you believe in divorce?"

With a surprised look on his face, Father Kaiser said, "Absolutely not. Why do you ask?" I told him that if I didn't get home for my anniversary pretty soon, he would be responsible for one. He laughed and said, "Please go home to your wife. We certainly can do this tomorrow." I thanked him and wrapped up the session.

For a couple of seasons, I assisted Bill Kendall on a showed called *Hee Haw*. After doing the show for two seasons, he decided that he wanted to move on to do other shows. I figured that would be a good time for me to quit the show also; it was a tough show to assist on because every edit (approximately 230 edits per show) required a reel change, and that's a lot of lifting of two-inch, ninety-minute reels. We went to Charlie, our boss, and told him how we felt. After thinking about it, he informed us that he could let Bill off the show, but he couldn't let off both of us. He had to have one person who knew the show. He said to me, "If you stay, I'll move you over to the editing chair." I thought it was a great opportunity to get my first network editing credit.

The following season I edited *Hee Haw*. Moving over one chair from assistant editor to editor on a network show was tougher than I thought. As the editor you are responsible for all the decision-making about how the show is edited. You get the credit when everything goes well, and you get the blame for anything that goes wrong. The editor is responsible for making sure that the show is edited in time for all airdates.

I soon realized what kind of pressure the editor was under. What made it much easier was the fact that Steve Cunningham was my assistant, and he was one of the best. He had a great sense of humor. During one of the editing sessions, as I bent over to move a reel of tape, my back snapped, and I couldn't move. Steve, who was built like the Hulk, picked me up, carried me to the car, and drove me home. He walked up to my front door carrying me in his arms like a baby and rang the doorbell. When my wife answered the door, the look on her face was priceless. We started to laugh and told her what had happened. She was great; Steve set me on the couch, and Carole Ann took care of me as usual. Steve and I finished out the season editing *Hee Haw*.

One day when I was at work talking to Carole Ann on the telephone, our home doorbell rang. I waited on the other end of the line while she went to the door. It was a telegram delivery. She opened it; I heard a loud scream, and then Carole Ann yelling, "You've been nominated for an Emmy!" We were both surprised and shocked that I was nominated for my first network show. Getting informed of your nomination by telegram—those were the good old days!

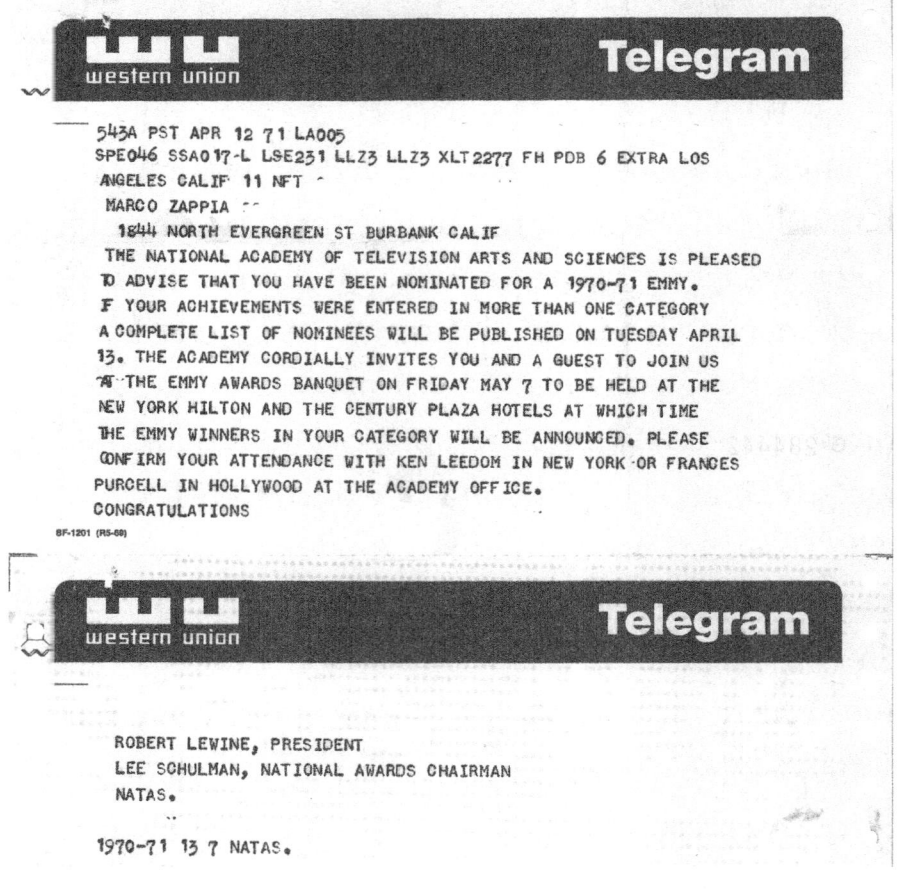

The night of the awards we got all dressed up, got a baby-sitter for our five-year-old daughter and one-year-old son, and off we went with the attitude that we would never win, but at least we would have a night out and a free dinner. *Hee Haw* was up against a Goldie Hawn special and a Hallmark Hall of Fame version of *Hamlet*. At the event, we were seated at a table with people who had won multiple Emmys.

The presenters for the editing category were Michael Constantine from the sitcom *Room 222* and Lori Saunders from the sitcom *Petticoat Junction*. When I heard them announce, "The Emmy goes to Marco Zappia for editing *Hee Haw*, you could have knocked me over with a feather. I couldn't remember a word that I said when I went up and accepted. When I got back to the table, everyone congratulated me. My wife was so excited she ran to the phone to let the kids, my mother-in-law, and everyone else in the family know that I had won. (The crafts and technical awards were not televised.) All in all, it was a pretty good night.

PRESENTERS: MICHAEL CONSTATINE AND LORI SAUNDERS

When I went back to work that Monday, everybody congratulated me. Charlie, my boss, told me that this was the first Emmy CBS had ever won for videotape editing, and he would like to keep it at CBS on display. I said, "If you can take it away from my wife, you can have it." Needless to say, he didn't ask me for it again.

Before the new season started, CBS cancelled Hee Haw, along with the rest of what they called their "hillbilly shows": *The Andy Griffith Show*, *Green Acres*, *The Beverly Hillbillies*, and *Petticoat Junction*, even though they were on the Neilsen ratings top ten list. They didn't want to be known as the "Hillbilly Network" any longer. This was a decision that I thought was fascinating—canceling five of their top-rated shows to avoid being known as the "hillbilly network."

I wanted to edit as much as I could, so I asked my boss if he could just give me shows that no one else wanted to edit. I figured that these were the shows that I could learn from the most. I still did some assisting; I felt there was still much more I could learn from the other editors. I cut a lot of religious shows and game shows. This experience allowed me to learn more about the equipment and how to deal with clients as the editor.

Always be willing to learn by going back and doing beginner jobs. You might learn something new or remind yourself of something you may have forgotten. Take jobs that you think you're beyond doing; you'll be surprised at what you will learn

The late 1960s and 1970s was a time when technology was changing fast. I was glad to be there when it all started. Every time we figured out how to do something that wasn't done before it was ground breaking. I remember assisting Bill Kendall on a *Budweiser Variety Special* starring Don Rickles, Don Adams, Edie Adams, and Charlton

Heston. The director, Grey Lockwood, wanted to end the show with Charlton Heston getting hit in the face with a cream pie and then freeze the shot. The Budweiser executives didn't think it was dignified to play that kind of gag on a star with Mr. Heston's stature. So the director told Mr. Heston what he wanted to do, and Mr. Heston said, "I love it; let's do it."

A simple freeze-frame or slow motion wasn't that simple in the '70s. We used the Ampex 100 videodisk, which was mainly used for sports events to get slow motion, instant replay, and freeze-frame effects. We had to hook up an oscilloscope to both the tape machine and the Ampex 100 and then time them together electronically. When this was done properly, we could make an edit from the disc to the tape machine without any glitches.

The fact that the time code couldn't be used to trigger the disc to freeze at the right time meant I had to anticipate the edit point and freeze the disc manually. I watched to see where the exact edit point would be and then when I matched it with the exact time code number, I pressed the freeze button. It took a couple of tries, but after I figured out my reaction time from where the specific time code of the edit hit to when I pushed the button, I was able to get it right every time.

Without today's technology, we had to rely on our inventiveness, technical knowledge, and a lot of prayers to come up with ways to try to accomplish what the directors wanted.

My boss decided that he wanted me to learn how to do the instant replay for the live football games. So he sent me to one of the Los Angeles Rams games at the coliseum to work with Len Labby, one of the editors there. In the remote truck where all the equipment was housed, Len said to me, "Why don't you observe me for a while, and I'll explain what I'm doing as we go along.

We did the instant replay and built the halftime package from the remote trucks. Sports shows were still being edited with a razor. Thank God that while I was teaching the other editors electronic editing, they taught me how to edit tape with a razor. I knew that, even though electronic editing would become the standard, it would be a while before physical editing was phased out, and I figured it wouldn't hurt to know how to make physical edits. That knowledge really paid off because, even though we were editing shows electronically, we still made physical splices in the master tape for some fixes to avoid going down a generation. (A generation is when you make a copy of the tape the quality is not as good as the original that's called the second generation. When you make a copy from the copy the quality is even worse so and so on.

The director and all the production people worked out of a different remote truck. During the game we recorded every play and wore headphones so that the director, through the assistant director (AD), could tell us which plays to save and which plays to rewind and record over. We recorded over the plays we knew we wouldn't be using in the halftime package. This practice made it much easier to edit the halftime plays together. Sometimes on a particular play we were asked to do an instant replay for the TV audience. It was fast and hectic to keep track of which plays to save and which to record over.

About twenty minutes into that first game, Len asked me if I would like to give it a try. I said, "Well, sure I'd be glad to." Boy was I nervous, but I jumped right into it. It sure was nice having him there to back me up if I needed him because, as it turned out, I did need his help several times, and he was glad to give it.

Five minutes before halftime, they told me to go ahead and put together the halftime package. I rewound to the first play and spliced together all the plays that I had saved, while taking out all the unneeded footage in between the takes. All the while I was editing, the AD was yelling in my earpiece: "How much time before you're finished?" The halftime announcer was on the air talking about the game, and he had to stall until I finished editing the half-time tape. I didn't have time to check the splices. The first time I knew if they played properly was when I saw them on the air. Thank God they all played through with only slight glitches.

When the playback was finished, we would save all the plays and then get ready to build and do replays for the second half. After I did a couple of more games, Tony, the director, requested that I do all the Rams games. I told him that there was a problem in that I didn't know the game very well. When I was in the game truck and was asked if I had recorded a certain player, I had to yell over the intercom to the AD "Give me a number, pal; I don't know one player from the next!" He laughed and said, "Zappia, you're one of my best replay guys, and you don't even know the game."

Maybe not knowing the game was a good thing. I could watch the game and do my job without being distracted by an interest in the plays.

One day during the off-season, some guy walked into the editing department with a half-inch reel-to-reel Sony videotape machine. His name was Hal Collins; I'll never forget him. He wanted someone to help him patch his machine into the racks so he could record one of the game show pilots. The audio and video racks were at the end of the videotape room. Any piece of audio/video equipment could be patched from the studios upstairs.

He wanted the same time code we recorded on the two-inch tapes burned into the video of his half-inch tapes. CBS at that time was a signatory of the IBEW (International Brotherhood of Electrical Workers) union. None of the guys wanted to help him. They said, "He's not a union member, and his machine could be just another tool depending on what it was going to be used for, that could take some jobs away."

Because of my curiosity, I volunteered to help him. I wanted to know what he was going to do with the tapes after he recorded them, so I asked him. He explained that he was going to screen the tapes with the producers. He would write down the time codes of where they wanted edits and create a paper edit list. He would then give the list to the editor who could then dial the numbers into the system and edit by the numbers.

This process was similar to the paper edit list I started making on the *Rose Parade Show* when I was assisting Lew Smith. Back then the edit list was strictly a backup reference in case we had to make any repairs or changes. However, Hal Collins wanted the producers to do all the viewing of their shows on a half-inch tape machine in a little room, instead of on the two-inch machines where the hourly rate was very costly. The written edit list created by these viewings was then used to assemble the show.

I thought, "What a great tool this could be for videotape editing." This occasion was the start of a crude offline system by which the editor and director could go into a room with three or four of these machines equipped with visual time code and, as the tapes were viewed, compile a paper edit list. On one machine the editor could freeze on the outgoing edit (where you want to make the edit to the master). On the other machine, the editor could freeze on the incoming edit (where you want to start from the playback machine and splice it to the master). Then the editor could compare the two frames to see how close he could get to a match of body position and action. The edit would then play through as if a different version never existed. The edit list was then taken to a different room, which was referred to as the online room. The master was then built on two two-inch high quality videotape machines.

I worked a lot with Hal Collins after that. At one time he was a writer for *The Milton Berle Show*, so he knew a lot about comedy timing. I asked him how he timed a joke for a laugh when there was no live audience. He said to just think of the old comedians like Jack Benny who put his hand on his chin and gave that great look into the camera to allow for the laugh, or George Burns who puffed on his cigar. Red Skeleton took a beat while he giggled or laughed at his own joke.

Because of Hal Collins' little machine, offline rooms developed that had several half inch tape machines with a monitor for each one. Each take was loaded on a different machine. This process allowed us to view one take after another. After the paper edit list was made, the online editing went much faster. This meant that more shows could be booked into the edit bays.

Remember: If you get a chance to help someone, do it. You may get a lot more back than you gave. Because of Hal, I learned a great deal about comedy timing and how his crude offline machine would help to advance videotape editing.

In 1971 a new sitcom called *All in the Family* was to be shot and aired at CBS. Norman Lear was the executive producer, and John Rich was the director. It was the first four-camera comedy shot on videotape. The show was shot in front of a live audience like a play. The CBS crew shot two performances: a dress rehearsal and an air show, each one in front of a different audience. If something didn't work for the dress audience, rewrites were done for the air audience. A live-switched feed (the director switching from camera to camera for different angles) was recorded, as well as a feed that would isolate different cameras at different times.

Jim Steiner was the editor on the first thirteen episodes of *All in the Family*. After Jim did his viewing in the offline room, he built the master. Jim asked me to assist him, and I was glad to do it. This offer gave me a chance to learn how a multi-camera show was edited. The assistant director, Bob Lahendro, sat with us during the editing process, so I got to know him quite well, too.

This show got some of the biggest laughs I had ever heard, but when you crossed performances (cut from dress rehearsal, for example, to a take from the air show), the laughs sounded, "Chopped." At that time there wasn't any way to blend the laughs. After the first thirteen episodes aired, the ratings were pretty bad. CBS wasn't sure whether they were going to pick up the show for another season. However, the network re-ran the show during the following summer, and word of mouth caused interest to grow, so CBS decided to renew the show.

Before the second season started, Jim went to work at the local Los Angeles CBS station. As a result, the show became available to other editors, but not many wanted to work with John Rich because he was such a perfectionist.

John started as an associate director when everything on TV was live. One day the director of a drama got sick, and John convinced the producers that he could step in and direct. From then on he was a director but he turned to comedy. He directed shows starring Jimmy Duarante, Ed Wynn, and Eddie Cantor. John was probably one of the best sitcom directors around. He really knew comedy and he really knew how to form the actors into their characters.

Bob Lahendro, the AD, went to Norman Lear and said, "I'd like Marco to edit the show." But my boss told Norman that I didn't have enough experience. Bob then told Norman that he'd rather have me with my lack of experience than any of the really experienced editors because he knew I could do the job, and I had the right personality to work with John. Norman agreed, but he said to Bob, "I hope you're right about this guy."

In those days the editor recorded not only the dress rehearsal and the air show, but also a few "pick-ups" (bits of scenes the producers or director wanted to do one more time). Overnight the tapes were dubbed to the half-inch tapes with a time code burned into the video that matched the two-inch tapes.

I didn't meet John Rich until the day after the first show when he came in for the viewing. Bob introduced me to him, and we got started. The routine throughout the season was that, with the script in front of us, we would view the tapes one page at a time. First we would watch the air performance and then the dress. John would decide which lines he wanted from dress and which from air. We would go through the whole show, and I would mark his performance notes in the script.

My assistant, Andy Zall, and I would then build our two-inch master using John's notes. Bob would be with us throughout the editing process because the presence of an assistant director was required by the Directors Guild of America (DGA)

The following day John would come down to the edit room with Bob to view our cut. He would give us his notes on performances and pacing, and if the show ran long, he would tell us what to cut. He would then say thanks and walk out of the room. I didn't really know if I were doing a good job or not because John never said much.

To prevent from going down a generation when we had to do any pull-ups in the scene, Andy and I made the changes using physical splices. At that time the two-inch tape machines did not maintain quality with generation loss. There were times in an electronic-generated master that I made five or six splices. We played the master on several machines until we found one that played our splices with the least glitches. We always made sure to use that machine when we had to make our air copies.

At one typical viewing, after I played two different takes for a page, John made the call saying, "Use air for these lines and then cross over to dress for the rest of the page." I said OK and started to mark the script. Then to my surprise, John yelled out, "What do you mean 'OK'? Don't you want to know why these are the better performances? Do you want to be a button pusher all your life, or do you want to be a creative editor?"

I said, "Creative editor." John then told me to play dress and air for the next page and pick the performances myself. I was pretty nervous about doing it because the director always picked performances. Our only job was to figure out how to make it happen. I guess, in a sense, we really were just button pushers, but we did have to be creative on how to make the director's requests happen. So I played dress and air for the next page and picked the performances. When I was right, John would say, "OK, go on." But when I was wrong he would yell out, "That's wrong, shmuck!" and then he explained why. Needless to say, I was wrong a lot more than I was right. After a while I didn't know if my name was "Marco" or "Shmuck."

As time went on, I was right more than I was wrong. Bob said John had never let another editor get that involved in the editing process before. I think John loved to teach, and maybe he saw something in me that made him think he could make a good editor out of me. I was very lucky that John took the time with me. He also taught me about pacing. When I played a scene, he would ask, "What's wrong with the scene?" At first I couldn't see anything wrong until he pointed out all the pacing problems. John really did teach me how to become a creative editor.

Whenever we crossed performances, there was an abrupt change in the audio if the laughs weren't the same. In the '70s and '80s, there were two audio tracks on videotape, but one was used to record time code. This situation meant audio couldn't be recorded separately and blended. When the network people would come to view the cut, the chopped laughs always threw them. We'd explain that it was because of the edit, and it would be fixed in sweetening. (Sweetening is a process where the master is taken into an audio room, all the music cues are added, canned laughs are added where needed, and all audio fixes are done.) One day John asked me to try to find a way to blend the laughs across the edit points.

Whenever you work with a talent like John Rich, he will push you and your equipment beyond your limits; this motivation will drive you to become better at your craft. It's also why technology keeps advancing.

I thought about it for a while and decided I could record past the edit point to let the entire laugh go by. Then when I went back to make the edit, I would somehow defeat the audio erase head across the edit point. As a result the laugh would blend, creating a smooth edit. I came up with a very simple solution to defeat the audio erase: I took a CBS label, folded it in half, and held it between the tape and the erase head. At exactly the right time, I quickly pulled the label out, and voila—the laugh blended with the incoming audio. It was crude, but it worked.

I like to compare the way we did things in those days to the difference between watching television and listening to the radio. When you listened to the radio, you had to rely on your imagination to put what you were hearing visually in your mind. To do what the director wanted, even though we didn't have the technology, we had to use imagination and ingenuity. You'll be surprised what might come to you if you do that.

All in the Family was cutting-edge comedy in those days. Some of the story lines were very controversial. I remember having to review one of the shows with John, Norman, and the network executives over what today seems something very simple: the sound of a toilet flush.

Watching John and Norman work the networks executives at those viewings was magical. John would start out like a bull in a china shop, complaining quite loudly about the network wanting them to take out the toilet flush and the profanity. Norman would then step in and say to John, "It's OK, John. Let me talk to them." Very calmly Norman would explain to them why he thought it was important for the toilet flush to stay in. The whole tone of the room changed, and soon Norman had them eating out of the palm of his hand.

Norman also always put something in the show that he could bargain with, like a "hell" or a "damn." Then he would say, "You're right about the profanity, and we'll take it out. The network executives agreed, and the viewing ended with everyone happy. Like the MasterCard Commercial says, **"It was priceless."**

I had already won an Emmy by the time I met John, but I never stopped learning my craft. Every year of my career I got better. John always said that I would never be nominated for an Emmy for editing *All in the Family* because of how seamlessly the show was edited. This opinion taught me something all editors should remember:

A good editor should cut a show so that it doesn't look edited.

John Rich did more for my career than anyone else. Every time the show won an award, and *All in the Family* won plenty, John would always thank me, whether it was in print or on the air. He called me his French Re-weaver because of how seamlessly the show was edited. John always said he considered me the Dean of Editing. Coming from John, that was quite a compliment.

These are some of the things I learned from John that are worth remembering:

- Think past your equipment and your abilities.

- Learn what story the script is trying to tell. (This is important because, through editing, you must make sure that the story is told.)

- Learn all about each character involved so that you can pick performances that reflect those characters.

- Understand that the editing dialogue is like editing music—everyone talks with a different cadence, and if you listen for it you'll be able to cut in between words, syllables, or even letters.

CHAPTER THREE

NEW PROJECTS
NEW CHALLENGES

I n 1973 I did a pilot for Lily Tomlin called *Lily*. Bill Davis, the director, had worked with me on *Hee Haw*. Lily and her partner, Jane Wagner, were very easy to work with. They appreciated any help I could give them. I really wanted *Lily* to get picked up as a series because of her great talent.

The show included a controversial sketch between Lily and Richard Pryor in which they answered a race-related questionnaire and, at the end of the sketch, Lily and Richard kissed. CBS wanted the sketch cut out of the show—remember, this was the seventies. Lily insisted the scene stay in. We made several other cuts to bring the show to time. CBS aired *Lily* as a special, but despite the high ratings, the network never aired it again, and the show was never made into a series.   Nonetheless, I got a very nice letter from Lily thanking me for my work on the show.

L.T.

Dear Marco,

I can never thank you properly for all your time and effort not to mention your patience with me and the show.

You were wonderful with us.

Love,

Lily

X

In 1975 CBS installed the CMX editing system. CMX was a joint venture between CBS and Memorex. CMX pioneered integrating computers with videotape editing. All editing was done at a keyboard with the actual editing machines either in another room or behind sliding glass doors just outside the room. On the old system you loaded the tapes and cued up to a certain time code. You could then rock the tape across the audio head to get right on the word or syllable. You felt that you had control of the accuracy of the edit. On the CMX system, your assistant loaded the tapes, and your contact with the tape was through the keyboard. The machines were completely out of your reach. It took some time to get used to this setup.

I finally realized what the editors meant when they said that they missed the physical contact they had by putting their hands on the tape.

When you wanted to make an edit, you first played your playback tape and, when the edit point came up, you hit the mark-in key on the keyboard. Thus your edit point was marked. How close you were to the actual edit point depended on your reaction time. You could preview the edit several times, adjusting the edit a frame at a time until it was correct. I couldn't use my trusty CBS label any more to blend the laughs. However, because I had enough technical knowledge to be dangerous, I asked Paul and Roger, in the maintenance department, if they could hook up a button that, when pressed, would electronically disable the erase head until the button was released.

Paul and Roger were the best. They came up with a way to do it. A dummy load was placed parallel to the erase head so that, when the button was pressed, the current was transferred to the dummy load until the button was released. A wire with a red button attached to the end of it ran from the machine to my console so that I could use it. I no longer needed my CBS label.

Whenever a new edit system was introduced, some of the editors had trouble learning it—so much so that they couldn't concentrate on their editing.

Once again I'll remind you that it is very important that you learn the tools of your craft so well you could use them without even thinking about it. You can then edit with confidence and concentrate on the creative side of editing.

Alan Blye, one of the top variety show producers once said to me that he was worried about getting the show done on time. I said, "Just sit back and relax Alan. It'll get it done in time."

Relieved, he replied, "Zappia, if this building were on fire and you told me not to worry, the fire will never get to us, I'd just sit here." I sure wouldn't trust me that much, but it did show that he was confident and relaxed.

You, the editor set the tone of the room. If you show confidence, everyone else in the room will also feel confident.

One day my boss came to me to ask if I would meet with some CBS and Sony engineers who were flying up from New York. They wanted to design a tape machine for the offline rooms that could be interfaced with the CMX 50 systems. This new machine would allow us to build a work print with a computerized edit list that could be fed into the online room edit system without having to insert the numbers manually. They wanted some input from me because I was doing two of the top shows—*All in the Family* and *Maude*.

When we met, the CBS and Sony people told me to tell them what I thought the machine should do, no matter how far-fetched I thought it was. I spent most of the day with them in an edit bay. I even showed how an edit sounded with the laugh cut off, and then with the laugh blended by pressing the red button releasing the load off the audio erase head to let the laugh record through until I realized the button. They were amazed at the difference.

After a couple of months, my boss told me that the machine they ended up designing was a one-inch tape machine that was too good for an offline room. Remember that the offline room was where the work print was built. It was a small room with much cheaper machines, so the picture quality was poor, but the room rates were a lot less than the online rooms.

The design ended up being the one-inch helical scan C machine, and this version replaced the two-inch machines in the online rooms. The BVH 1000 C machine was introduced in 1976 WHICH MENT we were still stuck with the half-inch Sony machines in the offline rooms. However, approximately six months later, we acquired new videotape machines. They were the Sony 5000 three-quarter inch Umatic cassette tape machines that could record and read time code and could be interfaced with the new CMX online system.

We installed five of these machines, so we were able to isolate each camera and record its feed on individual tapes. For editing, we needed five machines to stay in sync at a l times. Recording the same time code on all the reels achieved this synchronization for us. Having the individual cameras isolated made editing more flexible. If we had to cross performances on a line, the shot would be in the clear most of the time. Because the cameras were isolated during the whole show, we always had good reaction shots.

After the show was recorded, it was transferred to the three-quarter inch tapes with matching time code in the video and on one of the audio tracks. This process would allow us to do all the creative work in the offline room and edit the show to exactly what the producers wanted. A copy was then sent to the network executives for their notes. Afterwards we made the final version. Sometimes by the time the editor, the director, and the producers did their cuts, and the network people gave us their notes, the tape would be down four or five generations. With each generation, a time code was added from the record machine. Because of the quality of the three-quarter inch tapes, the cut was very grainy with several time code sources on the screen.

We used a program called the 409 to merge all the edit lists from the different cuts. Each edit list was fed into the system; then the new clean edit list was transferred to a punched Teletype tape. After a while came the floppy disc, which was fed into the edit system in the online room. The system automatically assembled the show to match the work print to the exact frame in a few hours.

This system was a great technology breakthrough. Instead of spending time to write down time code for each edit and then, in the online room, dialing the numbers into the machines, we were then able to spend more time on the creative process.

During one season we were doing so many shows at CBS that we didn't have enough machines in the building to accommodate them. CBS had to park one of its remote trucks with three tape machines and all the other equipment alongside the building where the audience stood in line to see *All in the Family.*

One night when I was getting ready to record one of the episodes of *All in the Family*, I noticed that the audience had already gone in, but there were three people still standing outside. I asked them why they weren't inside with the rest of the audience. They told me there weren't enough seats, so some people had to be turned away. They said, "We're from the Midwest and we really wanted to see the show before we went back." I told them that I couldn't help them get seats inside, but if they wanted to sit in the truck, they'd be welcome. I explained that they would be able to see the show and learn a little about some behind-the-scenes stuff. They jumped at the chance. I sat them to one side where they wouldn't be in the way but still could see everything that was going on.

I told the visitors how the equipment in the truck worked. I said, "The studio and I communicate with each other by intercom." I had an extra script for them to read, and I told them that they would see everything on the monitors that the audience was seeing. Then we heard the technical director's voice through the speakers: "Roll tape." I rolled both machines and then pressed record on each of them. When the tapes were up to speed, I answered back, "Tape speed."

Throughout the night I was in communication with the crew, who would always explain to me what they were going to do next. After shooting a particular pickup, John Rich, the director, asked me if I could make it work, and I answered that it was perfect. There also was a lot of kidding around between Bob Lahendro, the Assistant Director, and me. My small audience could hear any direction given to the actors about changes in lines or action. The director would tell the stage manager, who then told the actors. The audience couldn't hear any of this because they didn't have access to the intercom communication. At one point Jean Stapleton got on the intercom and asked how my family was doing. Almost every week she would ask me about my family. She is a wonderful, caring person.

After the show was over, my little audience was thrilled to death. They told me that they were glad they didn't get in because it was a lot more interesting being in the truck. They loved hearing the interaction between me, the director, and other people in the booth (a glass-walled room inside the studio where the director and the camera switcher worked, giving directions to the camera opera-tors and actors down on the stage). My audience espe-cially enjoyed hearing me chat with Jean Stapleton. I let them keep the script as a souvenir. They thanked me and left happy people.

In one episode of *All in the Family* that I edited, Edith was going through the change. There was a shot of her chasing Archie around the living room and dining room. The shot must have lasted twenty seconds, and it was all on one camera. All the while, Edith had dialogue and the laugh was huge. The problem was that the camera move wasn't very smooth, and sometimes it went out of focus.

That's what I love about editing shows that are shot in front of an audience. The audience energizes the actors, and they play off their laughs.

The following week we had to do a pick-up on the "Change" episode. Doing a pick-up a week later without an audience is very tough. Playing the scene with the same energy and making the action match to fit the laughs is nearly impossible for most actors. I played back the scene so that Jean could see what she had to do. She watched it a couple of times and said, "Let's do it." Jean did it so well that we recorded it only twice. The next day I pulled that episode and dropped the pickup in video only, just to see how far off it was and, believe it or not, one of the takes was in dead sync. All the original laughs and dialogue were saved.

Jean Stapleton was a real professional. She is the kind of actor who makes my job so much easier.

In one of the scripts, the writers introduced a new character: Edith's cousin Maude, played by Bea Arthur. The audience and CBS loved her so much that they created a new series called *Maude*, so Norman Lear had two shows on the air. One of the other editors cut this series, but on the eighth or ninth episode Norman Lear came to me and said, "We're doing a two-part episode of *Maude* on abortion and, because of the importance of the subject matter, we want you to cut both parts one and two." Hal Cooper, another high-powered sitcom director, was directing *Maude*. Norman and Hal were both so pleased with the way these two episodes turned out that they wanted me to be the permanent editor on the show. Of course, I said I would, but I was still editing *All in the Family*, and CBS had a policy that no editor could cut more than one show at a time.

Bob told me that Norman flew to New York to talk to Bob Woods, the president of CBS, and told him that if I didn't edit both shows, he would pull the editing out of CBS and do it elsewhere. Since Norman had two shows in the top ten for CBS, needless to say, I was soon cutting both shows. CBS had one stipulation: my assistant had to be an experienced editor so that, if anything happened to me, he could take over. Not many editors wanted to merely assist another editor, but   Jay Cook, who was a very good editor and a hell of a nice guy, agreed to do it. He assisted me on both shows. We worked a lot of hours, but Jay had a great personality, and he made it fun. Norman went on to shoot more pilots and, before you knew it, he had six shows in the top ten: *All in the Family*, *Maude*, *The Jeffersons*, *One Day At A Time*, *Good Times*, and *Sanford and Son*. I edited three of the pilots and the other four series were assigned to other editors.

June of 1972 THE IBEW union contract was up with CBS. We were in negotiations with them for six months without any of our demands being met by CBS. In June of that same year, IBEW called a strike against CBS over salary and benefit disputes. All the technical personnel walked out. June was the month when all the shows stopped taping for three months, and management could run everything else. Some mistakes were made on the air, but not enough to make a difference.

The union members took turns walking the picket line. Some of the production people and secretaries were very supportive. Throughout the day they would bring us coffee, donuts, snacks, and drinks. However, the people on the streets were not very happy with us. Women especially would walk up to us and yell, "Go back to work! We're missing our soap operas!" The day after Christmas, IBEW decided we should end the strike. We went back to work for exactly what the network had offered us six months earlier.

While we were on strike, CBS taped an episode of Maude with management operating the cameras. The episode was called, "Maude Bares All." It took place in a psychiatrist's office, and even though Maude sat on the couch during the whole episode, there were still camera problems. Sometimes the cameras would adjust and move in the middle of Maude's dialogue. In those days you would never use a camera that could adjust like that, but today they call it a style. That is something I just can't get use to.

I'm not saying it's a bad thing, but I feel as if I'm watching home movies that were taken by my kids. Besides, I picked the best performances whether the cameras were moving or not. That year the *Maude* show was nominated for best show, best script, and best director. I believe this was largely due to Bea Arthur's performance.

Remember, the editor's job is to protect the actor, and the best performances should be picked over anything else.

When the regular shows were on hiatus, CBS would assign me to edit musical variety shows such as *Tony Orlando and Dawn*, *The Glen Campbell Goodtime Hour*, *The Joey Heatherton Show*, *The Diahann Carroll Show*, and many more. I worked with some of the best variety show directors in the business: Mark Warren, Bill Davis, Art Fisher, Sterling Johnson, and John Moffat, to name a few. I was very lucky because, early in my career, I worked with some of the top people in the industry. As time went on, I guess I built up quite a reputation because people would request me more often than other editors to edit their shows.

I realized that no matter what you do in life, it would later help you with your career. I play a couple of musical instruments, which helped me cut musical variety shows. I majored in math, and that helped me to deal with all the time code numbers. I upholstered car seats, and my mom, dad, and I were the first to make car floor mats out of carpet. You might ask how making floor mats helped me. Well, when you place a pattern on the material, you have to place each piece carefully to get the most out of a piece of material—a lot like getting the most out of the footage that was shot and cutting it so that it worked as well as possible. (Hmmm well maybe that's a stretch).

I remember editing with Sterling Johnson, on several of Perry Como's Christmas specials and many other variety shows. When he wanted to adjust an edit, he had his own way of expressing the increments. I had a frame reference guide I used when editing with Sterling. When he said to tighten or loosen an edit a bit, that meant a frame or two. When he said to adjust the edit a tad, this could be a three or four frame adjustment. When he said a bunch that meant, "Are you kidding me?" Fix that damn edit!"

During one of the hiatus periods, I did a pilot for Rob Reiner called *Sonny Boy* that he had written with his partner. Rob also directed the pilot, and even back then he was a very talented director. My wife bought me a pair of suede boots for my birthday before I started editing. I decided to wear the boots to work only when I started a new show or edited a pilot. It was something I did just for luck. One day while we were editing, Rob said, "I really like your boots. I'd like to get a pair. Where'd you get them"? I told him my wife bought them at Sears. A couple of days later he came in with a pair, and he proudly showed them to me. I think that was the same pair he wore in the episode of *All in the Family* in which he and Carroll O'Connor did the famous sock and shoe routine. The rest of the session went very well. Rob was a nice guy and a pleasure to work with.

During the holidays, and at the end of each production season, the producers threw huge cast and crew parties. I never attended because I just didn't feel comfortable at these affairs. When we recorded *All In The Family's* one-hundredth episode, Norman Lear threw a party at the Bistro restaurant in Beverly Hills. All the cast and crew were invited. I told Norman that I wouldn't be attending because I didn't feel comfortable at parties, and I didn't usually go. He told me that if my wife and I weren't at the party he was going to send a limousine to the house for us. Needless to say, we went.

We sat with all the editors working on Norman's other shows; they also brought their wives. Throughout the night Norman would take me around and introduce me to all the big CBS brass. He would say to them, "This guy is the reason I'm doing my shows at CBS." That was kind of embarrassing.

On one *All In The Family* episode, Norman hired a director whose only experience was directing soap operas. After we did all our cuts, Norman came to the edit bay to view the show. After the viewing we asked him if he were going to hire that director again because we didn't think he was very good. I told Norman that show had been one of the toughest ones I had ever edited because of that man's directing. Norman turned to me and said, "The show turned out great. It looks like he gave you everything you needed to edit." He then smiled and walked out of the room.

Without saying it, Norman Lear told me, "The editor's job is to use whatever footage the director shoots and make it work."

One of the reasons CBS had such a great technical staff was that the network was always trying to improve the craft of broadcasting. Whether I was editing a sitcom or a variety show, after a show aired, the camera operators would come down to my edit bay to ask me questions about their shots. If one of their shots hadn't been in the show, they wanted to know why I didn't use it. I would pull that shot from the original reels to show them. Sometimes it was a focus problem, sometimes there was a bump in the shot, or sometimes the move wasn't very smooth.

I thought it was great when the camera operators came to my edit bay. Whenever I talked to them about their shots, it would always help me with my editing. For example, on sitcoms there were times when I would have liked to stay on a shot a little longer to allow for the laugh, or to let the person speaking finish his or her thought. But as soon as the red light on their cameras went off, the camera operators would immediately move to their next position, even though that shot wasn't needed for a couple of pages. I told them; if possible, after the red camera light went off, all I needed was for them to take a deep breath before they made their moves.

The response to that advice was great. Each week the camera operators would come to see me and ask, "How'd we do this week?" When they knew they had enough time, they would slowly follow the person on whom they had been focused back to the next shot. This effort gave us another shot to use if we needed it. These guys were becoming more creative with their camerawork, and the directors and I loved it.

Work together with the rest of the crew. While improving your craft, you will help them to improve theirs. This practice will also help make the show better. It's a win-win situation.

CHAPTER FOUR

MOVING ON TO
NEW ADVENTURES

After I had been at CBS for ten years, one of the producers, Alan Blye, wanted me to edit a big special for him, but the scheduling department told him that I wasn't available. Instead, I was slotted to degauss tapes in the vaults. One day I happened to meet Alan in the hallway. He told me that he had requested me to do his special, but they said I was working on something else. So I went to our crackerjack scheduling department to ask why they told Alan that I was working on another show when they had me just degaussing tapes. The scheduling department said, "There are no stars in the edit department!"

My problem with the situation wasn't the money. At CBS, whether you pulled cables, put shows on the air, or were one of the most-requested editors, we all got the same pay. My problem was, I just wanted to edit.

That evening when I got home, I told my wife what had happened and, without a beat, she said it was time for me to leave CBS. She was always very supportive, and her instincts were always right on. About a week later I got a phone call from CFI, a post-production facility in Hollywood. They wanted to meet with me about going to work for them. Carole Ann and I decided that if I could get close to double my salary, it would be worth making the move. At CBS I was making top pay, $320 a week, so if I got between $600 and $640, I would leave CBS.

I set up a meeting with Dennis, the operations manager of CFI. He gave me the tour of the facility. They had all the state-of-the-art equipment. When I went into the edit bays, I was surprised to see grass valley switchers—new technology I'd never worked with—in each bay. I commented on the switchers to Dennis, so he asked me if I was familiar with that particular switcher. "Very much so," I said, even though I had never touched one. At CBS we had no switchers in our bays; when we had to make a dissolve or a wipe, a transition between two scenes, we would use the CMX computer. I figured I could certainly learn to use the grass valley switcher…I hoped.

As we were walking through the hallways, I heard people saying, "That's him; I wonder if he's going to come and work here." I asked Dennis, "Who are they talking about?" He said, "You. Your reputation has preceded you." Boy, that surprised me. I didn't think anybody had heard of me; I was just working in the basement at CBS doing something I really loved.

We went to Dennis's office to discuss salary. I told him I needed $600 a week to make a move. He said he could only go as high as $585. I couldn't say yes right away because I didn't want to seem anxious, so I said I'd let him know. When I told my wife what happened, she laughed and said, "Break his arm and take it before he changes his mind." So the next day I called Dennis to tell him I would take the deal, and I gave CBS two weeks' notice.

It was a little sad leaving CBS. For the previous ten years I'd worked with and learned from some of the best editors in the business. As a crew, we worked together to improve our individual crafts, and we learned how to work around the lack of technology to do things that had never been done before.

We accomplished this innovation by using imagination and ingenuity.

In 1968 we gave up razor blades for computer keyboards to edit two-inch videotape in the space of a few years. In 1976 offline rooms were created from a one-half inch reel-to-reel Sony machine to a computer-based CMX system controlling three-quarter inch Umatic tape machines. A list could be generated to feed the online machines for an auto assembly. In 1976, the helical scan C machine was introduced and replaced the two-inch videotape machine. In 1971 we shot and edited the first four-camera sitcom at CBS, and I was fortunate enough to have worked with and learned from some of the industry's top producers and directors.

I was the first person to quit CBS in twenty-five years, employees only left after they retired, so most of the people were surprised. The videotape department gave me this large card saying, "You're going and we're staying," and they all signed it, wishing me luck. Jim Gothie, the commercial coordinator, made these great drawings for me that kind of summed up how they felt.

ART WORK BY JIM GOTHIE

ART WORK BY JIM GOTHIE

When I went to work for CFI in 1978, I encountered some equipment that I hadn't used before. At first, we weren't very busy, so CFI allowed the editors to stay home until we were needed. After about three or four days, I went to work, even though they hadn't called me. I thought I'd use the time to learn some of the equipment. CFI had two online bays. One was equipped with five two-inch machines controlled by a CMX editing system, and the other had five one-inch helical scan C machines controlled by a Mach One Editing System.

Jim Adams developed the Mach One. The software included the then unique concepts of an Active list and On-The-Fly sync roll.

Both rooms had grass valley 1600 video switchers. I knew how to operate the CMX editing system, so I spent time training myself on the Mach One editing system. The company hadn't come out with a user's manual for the Mach One yet, so I asked the engineers to give me a short lesson on how it worked.

Whenever you want information on any piece of equipment, the engineers can teach you the basics better than anyone else.

At that time there were five other editors working at CFI: Danny White, Chip Brooks, Mario DiMambrio, Don Johnson, and Art Schneider. The scheduling department had just booked Walt Disney's *The New Mickey Mouse Club*. We all took turns editing on the show. This job also gave me a chance to teach myself the video switcher. To learn more about the Mach One, I worked in the room with the Mach One edit system, when I had a chance.

When I wasn't busy, I asked the maintenance engineer if he could teach me how the offline room worked. The offline bay had five one-inch reel-to-reel machines controlled by a Mach One Editing System. Each machine had its own monitor. He told me that the other editors didn't like the Mach One very much, so the room was hardly ever booked. I said, "Once I learn to operate the equipment, I'm sure clients will be booked in the offline room before you know it.

One of the things I liked about the Mach One was that, because of the "Active List" and the "On-The-Fly" sync roll software, we could roll the four isolated-camera tapes in sync. At the same time, we could be recording on a fifth tape, switch to each camera from the keyboard, and generate an Active List. I wasn't crazy about the one-inch reel-to-reel machines. On a humid day we had to pour baby powder on the tape; otherwise the moisture in the air would cause the tape to stick together and prevent the machines from working properly. I really missed the three-quarter cassette tape machines we had at CBS in our offline rooms.

The first show I booked in the offline room was a sitcom called *We've Got Each Other* for MTM (the Mary Tyler Moore production company). It was a four-camera taped show, and it was shot at the CBS Radford Studios in Studio City, California. Because this was a film lot, the union didn't allow a technical director in the booth during taping. One member of the technical crew did a rough switched feed for the audience to watch on the monitors, but it wasn't recorded.

The day after the show was shot, I went to the studio and sat in the booth with the director and the assistant director. I rolled the four-camera tapes in sync and, as the director pointed to the monitor that matched the camera he wanted, I pressed the button on the switcher to cut in that particular camera. We recorded the switched feed on a fifth tape machine. We did this with both performances and any pickups. I could hear some of the film crew whispering "He's editing the scene while he's playing the tapes." I wish it were that easy, but actually my work had just begun.

I took the tapes back to CFI where they were first dubbed to the offline machines. I used the tape on which I had recorded the director's switched feed strictly for viewing the different takes and as a reference for where the director wanted to cut to the different cameras. When the switcher is used to cut in the cameras, an edit list is not generated. I viewed all the takes to see which take had the best performance. I then rolled the four-camera tapes in sync using the keyboard to cut to the proper camera. At the same time an edit list was being generated.

When editing on the Mach One, I was working with an active list; this allowed me to build the master up to the point where I wanted to change performances. I then cut in that performance and continued to build the scene with the preferred take. After I built each scene this way, I went back and fixed any late camera cuts and dropped in any reaction shots that were needed.

Now this is very important: because I'm a very nosy guy, I watched the whole scene one more time to see if I missed anything. It could be somebody reacting to what was said, or to a laugh, some physical activity that was happening, or something as simple as one of the characters entering the room off camera. (If you miss a character's entrance, then cut to the character speaking so the viewer wonders where the entering character came from.)

You have to make the people in the audience at home feel as if they are in the room with the characters.

After I finished my cut, the producers and director came to the edit bay to give their notes. By that time there shouldn't be many. A good first cut should be at least 85 percent of what they want, and the rest is very subjective. Once I made the changes according to the director's, producers', and network's notes, I took the floppy disc that contained my edit list into the online room to assemble the show.

My assistant was a guy named Jeff Male. The machines were on the other side of sliding glass doors and, after Jeff loaded the five machines with tapes, he sat next to the machines while I did my assembly. After a couple of episodes, I called Jeff into the room to ask him if he were planning to be an editor. He said, "Absolutely." I said, "If that's the case, then after the tapes are loaded and ready to go, you should come into the room with me and observe."

Jeff said, "The other editors don't allow the assistants to be in the room, especially if there are clients around." I told him when he worked with me he would not only be allowed in the room, I expected him to come in and learn all he could.

I said, "I feel the more you know, the more you will be able to help me." After that, Jeff and I had a lot of fun working together, and he turned out to be a top-notch editor. Jeff and his family became lifelong friends. Soon the other editors started to work with their assistants the same way.

One day while I was editing *We Were Meant For Each Other*, Nancy Heydorin, the assistant director, asked me if I could help out a friend of hers. His name was Will McKenzie, and he had just directed a play at Beverly Hills High School. She wanted to know if I could edit it for him on my own time. He was going to use the reel to get directing jobs for TV shows. I said, "I'd be glad to do it for him."

Will McKenzie was a character actor and a regular on the Bob Newhart TV series. Will also did commercial voice-overs. He was probably best known as the voice of the nose in the Alka-Seltzer commercials. A week later, after I finished my other work, Will came in, and we started editing his play. He's a nice guy, and we got along great. Since then he's become one of the top TV directors in the industry. I've worked with Will on shows such as *Soul Man*, *Archie Bunker's Place*, *Carole And Company*, *Father And Sons*, and *We've Got Each Other*.

As I said before, if you can help someone out, do it. It will always come back to you in a good way. In Will's case, I gained both a new friend and a very good client.

One of my old clients, Don Vanetta, brought a show to me called *Husband, Wives and Lovers*. It was a one-hour comedy shot with four cameras. I worked with some of the top comedy directors on this show, including Mark Daniels. He was one of the great directors on the *I Love Lucy* show along with Alan Myerson, James Burrows, and Bill Persky. Working with these directors was a great experience.

Mark Daniels taught me that the editor's job is to edit the show to protect the actors. If you had to choose between the perfect camera shot or the best performance, you have to go with the performance. The actor is on the screen, and the audience is watching his or her performance, not whether the shot is perfect. Mark said, "If the show happened to get cancelled, people will say that the actor's show was cancelled, not Marco's show was cancelled."

The first couple of episodes I assembled in the CMX room took six hours to complete. The machines stopped after each edit and re-cued for the next edit. I asked Don if he could book the Mach One room instead of the CMX room. He said that the CMX room was one hundred dollars an hour cheaper than the other room, and he couldn't justify paying the difference.

I thought if I could save some time, I would have more time for my other shows. I figured the best way to convince him was to show him. Out of desperation I assembled the next show with the Mach One System. When all the tapes were loaded and cued up, the Mach One would make each edit without stopping the machines. The assembly took three hours instead of six, saving the producers 600 dollars an episode. I also had three more hours to work on my other shows. When Don got the bill, he called me to ask why the bill was so much less. I told him it was because I used the more expensive room. He just laughed and said, "OK, you win." Sometimes you just have to do the math for them.

Unfortunately, after nine episodes aired, *Husband, Wives and Lovers* was cancelled. Most of the production staff went on to other shows, leaving me to cut the remaining episodes that had already been shot. It turned out to be an opportunity for me; I picked all the performances myself and got the shows ready to air.

Sometimes when things like cancellations happen, you see it as a negative. On the other hand, it can be an opportunity that allows you to use some of your other skills and expand the way you do your job.

One of my colleagues at CFI was Danny White, one of the top variety show editors around. He had edited a Barry Manilow special but, when Danny went on vacation, my boss asked me to step in for some further work with the special's producer. The producer wanted to end one of the acts sooner by making a music edit in one of the songs while keeping the fade-out the same. He showed me the area where he wanted to make the cut. I played it a couple of times, keeping in mind that I had to make a music edit and a clean video edit. After I checked it one more time, I made my edit. When I played it back for him, he said, "Wow, you're good—but you don't act like you are."

I said, "You telling me I'm good after I have worked with you is better than me saying it."

You can brag about yourself as much as you want, but it's how you treat your clients and how you do the job that builds reputations.

Rita Scott, a very nice lady and a dear friend, was a producer with whom I had worked at CBS when I was assisting Bill Kendall. She asked me to edit the Bette Midler special, *Old Red Head Is Back.* Dwight Hemmion, the director, had done some of the biggest variety specials on the air. Dwight didn't believe in the offline process. He thought of it as editing the show twice, so we went straight to online.

All during the editing process, Bette Milder would come in before Dwight to see how the show was coming out. I played one of the finished segments and she said, "Why are there all those close-ups of me during the song?" I told her that we couldn't play the whole song on a wide shot because people wanted to see her face while she was singing. She just said, "I still don't like the way I look in the close-ups." It always amazes me that no matter how big the stars are, they all have some insecurity.

Dwight wanted me to do something on the switcher that I didn't know how to do. I said, "I think I know someone who could help me." I brought Danny White into the room. Rita and Dwight had worked with Danny before and they knew he was an expert with the switcher. We told Danny what we were trying to do. He said, "You can't do that with this switcher, but you could take that section down a generation and do it that way."

The reason I tell this embarrassing story is so you remember not to be afraid to ask for help. The clients will appreciate the fact that you did everything you could for their show, and you might even learn something by asking.

Another incident at CFI occurred as I was finishing my last editing job of the day. Dennis, the operations manager, asked me if I could assist one of the other editors because that editor had a couple of hours work left but nobody else wanted to stay and help him finish. I told Dennis that I'd be glad to help. I always liked to assist every once in a while, just to keep my hands on the machines.

So I was sitting at the machines on the other side of the sliding glass doors when a voice came over the intercom—it was the editor asking me to change a reel. The sliding door was open enough for me to hear what was going on in the edit bay. The assistant director was in the room with the editor. She was giving both the director's and producer's notes to the editor. I couldn't see the AD's face, and I didn't know her name, but the editor was really giving her a bad time. When she tried telling him what she wanted, he either refused to do it because he was too lazy, or he just didn't agree with her. He was being very rude to her. I didn't think any client should be treated that way, especially a lady. I know the feminists would get on me for saying "especially a lady." I guess I'm one of those old-fashioned guys who still think women should be respected.

I hit the intercom key and asked the editor to come out of the room because I needed to ask him something about one of the reels. He came out, and I told him that if he didn't stop treating the AD so rudely and quit being such an ass, I would leave and he could put up his own reels. He just looked at me, and then went back into the edit bay. I guess he didn't want to lower himself by loading his own reels. For the rest of the session he was a perfect gentleman. (Well, at least he was civil.)

Remember, you should always treat everybody with respect, whether it's an assistant director or the production assistant on the show. It's the right thing to do. Besides, someday you might be working for that person.

I was editing a special called *Billy Graham in Poland*. It was about the holocaust. The viewer was taken through the concentration camps, and then actual footage was shown of the torture and killing of the Jews. This was some of the most horrifying footage I've ever had to watch. Because there was so much material to go through, I worked around the clock for several days. The assistant directors would come in shifts to work with me. In the midst of this work, I got a phone call, and the voice on the other end said, "Hi, I'm John Astin, actor, producer, and director. I would like to talk to you about coming to work for me." He said that he and his three partners were opening a new post-production facility.

When I heard his voice on the phone I recognized it immediately. It was Gomez Addams from the TV series *The Addams Family*. What a kick! I wanted to meet with him just so I could talk to him in person.

John's company was called Astin/Moore, and he wanted me to be his head editor. I did what I usually do when I had a tough decision to make: I went home and discussed it with my best friend and personal advisor, my wife. I told her about the conversation I had with John, and we decided that it wouldn't hurt to talk to him.

The next day I set up an appointment with John, and we met at his facility. It was kind of surreal talking to John—I felt as if I were actually talking to Gomez Addams. John was very charming, and he and his partners showed me around their facility. The editing system they used was a Mach One, which I thought was great. They had one offline room and one online room. The industry at that time was using C format one-inch tape machines. Astin/Moore was using B format one-inch tape machines. Bosch, a German company, built the one-inch B VTR, which had become the broadcast standard in Europe. However, in the United States, the C format VTR was much more successful.

I told John I didn't think he could get much business because I didn't know anyone who was shooting shows on B format. I said, "John, there are a lot of good editors out there who wouldn't cost as much as me to hire, and they would be glad to work for you. When your business gets busy enough for me to make a move, we can talk."

He said, "I want you because I did a survey with the top producers and directors in the industry. I asked them to name the four editors they would like to work with the most. Your name was the first name on the list of every producer and director I talked to. You're the one I have to hire if we're going to make the facility a success." I told him I'd get back to him.

So, once again, I discussed what John had said with my wife. I told her that because of the format I didn't think that my clients would follow me. She said, "This might be a great opportunity to get in on the ground floor of a new facility. We should stick to our plan, and if you could double your salary, make the move." I was making $35,000 a year, so I would have to ask for $70,000 a year, which I thought was way too much to ask for, mainly because I loved editing so much I would probably do it for nothing. Now you see why I leave the negotiations to the smart one of the family.

We then wrote down the amount we wanted. When Astin/Moore asked what it would take for me to go to work for them, I would just hand the paper to them. We also planned to ask them to pay a $25,000 sign-up fee that Carole Ann knew they would not want to pay. This would give me something to give up as a good will gesture.

I went back and met with Astin/Moore, and when they asked what it would take for me to go work for them, I handed them the slip of paper. After a look of panic on their faces and a huddle between them, they said that they could pay the salary but not the sign-up bonus. I don't know how Carole Ann does it, but she sure knows people. I told them I'd give up the sign-up fee, but I needed a month to make the move.

I went back to CFI and gave them two weeks' notice. I told Dennis that I still had a lot of work to do on the *Billy Graham Special*, so he needed to assign another editor to work with me who could take over the show. After two weeks I was surprised with a nice going-away party.

I worked at CFI only a short time—less than a year—but I learned a new editing system, The Mach One, and the grass valley switcher. I also got to work with some new clients and a nice group of people at CFI.

CHAPTER FIVE

EDITING WITH
NEW PROBLEMS

It was 1979 when I started working at Astin/Moore. Lori King answered the phones and did the scheduling of the edit bays. David Orr, the engineer, and Dave Moore was a partner and general manager. After I had worked there for about a week, I thought to myself, "What in the hell did I get myself into?" The equipment was constantly breaking down. To get through one session, we had to have one of the electronic boards on one of the tape machines pulled out on an extender so that someone could sit on the floor with a blower to keep the board cool. Dave Orr was working day and night, but no matter how hard he worked, nothing ever got really fixed because it was too much for one guy to handle. Our switcher was an old two-bank switcher. The one bright spot was the offline room; it was equipped with five three-quarter inch Sony Umatic machines that were controlled by a Mach One editing system that worked pretty well. I felt as if I had been beamed back in time to the land of bad technology.

Another company called Video One shared part of the building. It had a couple of production trucks that had B format machines to record whatever they shot. We did a lot of their commercials. If a client came in with C format tapes, we would transfer the material to our B format machines so that we would be able to edit that client's project.

After a couple of weeks of fighting faulty equipment, I went to the partners to tell them that we had to hire another maintenance person. After some arguing, they agreed. I called my brother Val who, at that time, was working for National Cash Register. He knew a lot about computers and electronics, and I knew he could figure out this equipment in no time. This was the time to surround myself with smart people that I knew and could trust. After a couple weeks of working on the equipment, Val and Dave Orr got the equipment working.

All I had to do then was figure out how to get clients to come to our facility to edit. When people saw the sign Astin/Moore on the building, they thought it was a car dealership. So the partners wanted to change the name to Astin/Zappia. I was well known in the industry, so there would be no doubt that we were a post-production facility.

ASTIN/ZAPPIA POST PRODUCTION FACILITY

Business started picking up as soon as the new sign went up, and the name change was advertised in the trade papers *Variety* and *The Hollywood*

Reporter. Of course, Carole Ann negotiated a pretty good partnership deal for me, too.

When some of my old clients called, I told them that we would transfer their material from C format to B format at our expense. We would then be able to edit their shows. We had only one edit bay, so they were still a little reluctant. If our edit bay went down for maintenance, they wouldn't be able to meet their airdates, so I worked out a deal with CFI. They would have an edit bay waiting for us at their facility if our edit room was down for any reason. Thank God that never happened.

Ad agencies are the toughest clients. They will take hours to decide where to bring in a simple graphic. If there were two or three clients in the room, they would constantly argue about where to place the graphic. As a result, I decided that I would handle such commercial clients a little differently.

While cutting a commercial for one of the big ad agencies from New York, I was at the console, and the clients in their suits and ties were sitting behind me, very quiet and probably bored. I was ready to place the graphics in the commercial, so I turned to them and said; "I'm ready to bring in the graphic now. Would one of you like to come up to the console and show me where you want it?" One of the gentlemen took off his coat and sat in front of the switcher. I said, "When you want the graphic to appear on the screen, just pull the handle on the switcher toward you and push it away to lose it." He looked at me, a little surprised. I said, "Don't worry, it's just to give me an idea of where you want to place the graphic. We can redo it if it's wrong."

I rolled the tapes, and he tried it. The guy was so thrilled: he wanted to do it again. He said, "I know I could do it better. I'd like to try it one more time." We did it again, and immediately the session became relaxed. They all wanted a turn. I was doing several versions of their commercial that day, so they each had a chance at the switcher.

I got to edit Michael Jackson's first video as an adult performer, *Don't Stop Till You Get Enough*. It was released in 1979, two years before the launch of MTV. It happened that we needed to work all through the night, and the producer asked me to make a lot of strange-looking edits. Not having edited music videos before, I figured that he knew what he was doing. He came in the next afternoon to view what we had done the night before. When he saw it, he went crazy. He yelled out, "That's not what I edited last night! We have to redo it."

I asked him, "Do you mean to tell me you don't remember the edit session last night?"

"I remember editing, but I certainly don't remember editing what you just showed me."

I knew he must have been stoned the night before by the way he was acting. I told him that we would come up with a price that would be fair to both of us to redo the spot, but he had to come in completely sober. At first he hesitated, and then he agreed. The next night he seemed to know what he was doing, the session went much faster, and the video turned out great.

I'm telling you about these clients to prepare you because there will be times when you will be working with some very difficult people. Every situation will be different, but you have to be able to handle it.

The first TV series that booked with Astin/Zappia was *Archie Bunker's Place.* Roxie Wink Evans was one of the producers; I had worked with Roxie for years at CBS. The show used various directors on different episodes. One particular week the director entered the edit bay and introduced herself as Linda Day. I greeted her like I do all directors, and we sat down. She then said, "You don't remember me, do you?"

I said, "No I'm sorry. Have we worked together before?"

"I was the assistant director who was in an edit bay at CF when you called the editor out of the room. I heard everything you said to him, and I'll never forget it. I've always wanted to thank you."

I said, "You're welcome. The guy was being such a jerk, I had to call him on it." After that, Linda and I worked together on a lot of projects.

In 1980 I did a special for the Captain and Tennille. Toni Tennille loved our little facility; she liked to call it "boutique editing." She liked all the personal attention they got. She got to know everybody in the facility and loved to visit.

No matter how small or large the facility is, you have to make the clients feel comfortable and secure in the fact that their project will be completed without any problems {a lot of prayers were said to cover that one}.

One day, Lee Hale, the producer of *The Dean Martin Comedy Hour*, came in to look over our facility. He liked the idea of working at a small facility, and he knew they would get a lot of personal attention, so Lee booked *The Dean Martin Comedy Hour* with us. Lee was a great guy to work with. First, we would offline the show for a few days. Then a couple of days later they came back with director Gregg Garrison's notes, which were pretty specific. We transferred the show's C format material to one-inch B format. When editing with the Mach One, you worked in an active edit list, so we could auto-assemble the show again up to where the change was to be made, type in the new numbers for the change, update the edit list, and continue the assembly until the next change. This process meant we didn't have to take the show down a generation to make the changes. The auto-assembly process on the Mach One was very quick, and we were able to go to the online room with a clean edit list.

Doing the Dean Martin show was huge to me. He was one of my all-time favorites. Back in my RCA TV repair days, I had a service call to go to Dean Martin's house in Beverly Hills to set up his new color TV set. When I got there, Dean was in the living room practicing twirling his gun. He called me into the room, did some tricks with the gun, and asked me what I thought. I told him that it was great. I asked him if he were preparing for a movie, and he said, "I'm going to do a western called *Rio Bravo* with John Wayne, Angie Dickinson, and Ricky Nelson." Who would have thought that almost twenty years later I would be editing his TV show? You never know what life will bring you.

One day the Mach One Company called me and wanted to know if they could interview me and take my picture. I didn't think much about it, and I said, "Sure." They came to the edit bay, asked me a couple of questions, and took a couple of pictures with me in front of the console. Before I knew it, that picture was in every broadcasting magazine in the country. In about a week, the Mach One people came back, and while I had a room full of clients, they said they needed me to sign something. Now I'm not making any excuses for having kidneys for brains that day, (well maybe I am) but I did have a room full of people.

When Carole Ann saw the ad in one of the magazines, she asked me, "Did you give them permission to use your picture?" Carole Ann must have seen the look on my face as I realized what I had signed because she immediately asked, "You didn't sign anything, did you?" I told her I "sort of" did; they brought me something to sign while I was editing, and I signed it without reading it." She then said, "Honey, I told you not to sign anything without me reading it first." Once again, she was right, and after that Carole Ann has read everything.

Since I was the only editor at Astin/Zappia, I had to edit every project that was booked. We started to get pretty busy, so I had Dave Moore hire Jeff Male, my assistant at CFI, to come to work for us. He was not only a great assistant, he was also a good editor who helped me with the auto-assembly of shows and edited some of the Dean Martin shows.

I remember when Allen Funt came in for an edit session. He was pitching the idea of bringing back *Candid*

Camera to network television. *Candid Camera* was a hidden camera series that initially began on radio as Candid Microphone on June 28, 1947. *Candid Camera* started on television on August 10, 1948, which Alan Funt produced and directed.

Allen Funt was to be the producer and director of the new *Candid Camera*. After his meeting with the network, he was not a happy man. Allen told me that the network executives were a bunch of young kids trying to tell him how to make a candid camera show. It would be like me trying to tell Frank Capra how to direct a movie.

I understood how he felt. When I did pilots for the networks, I found that the network executives were not much older than kids. I expected their parents to walk into the room to pick them up right after the viewing. Either these guys were getting a lot younger, or I was just getting older, or maybe a little of both.

Like most small companies, we all had to pitch in with everything. In the morning I stopped on my way to work and got the donuts, while Lori made the coffee and opened up the offices. Val, Jeff, Dave, and I made sure that the edit bays were working and ready. We also made sure the restrooms were clean.

After a while the clients weren't getting that personal service they were used to getting. Answering the phones, dealing with clients, billing and scheduling became too much for Lori to handle by herself. I turned to the only person whom I trusted with my life: Carole Ann. At that time she was working at an escrow company from 8:30 a.m. to 2:30 p.m., then picking up the kids from school. I asked her—well, maybe "asked" isn't the right word—I begged her to come to work at Astin/Zappia from 3:00 p.m. to 6:00 p.m. to see if she could figure out what was going on up front.

Carole Ann is one of the smartest women I know. She knows how to read people, so I knew she could straighten out the problem. She started out helping Lori answer the phones, and they became very good friends. The clients got to know Carole Ann really well, so whenever they had a problem they would go to her for help. Eventually, Carole Ann came to work full time, and I was able to concentrate strictly on my editing. She worked with the partners, management, and clients. I love being spoiled by that woman.

As I have said: "Surround yourself with people you can trust, and if they happen to be smart and talented, what the hell."

One day Fred Fuchs, the producer of Shelley Duvall's *Faerie Tale Theatre*, came to our facility. He asked Carole Ann if he could book time to edit one of their shows with us. He said, "Our editor is busy with another project and couldn't do it, but after this episode we'll take the show back." She told him that we would be glad to accommodate him.

Faerie Tale Theatre was a live action children's television series retelling popular fairy tales. Shelley served as narrator, host and executive producer of the series.

The episode I did was "Hansel and Gretel," directed by James Frawley. Jim directed many films as well as TV series shot on film. I was amazed at how well the show was lit. Everybody always said that the problem with videotape was that tape couldn't be lit as well as film. Tape was always lit very flat—sort of one-dimensional. However, for the first time, I saw tape lit as well as any film show. It was great. The show was shot with four cameras and sometimes a fifth camera up on a crane.

When the director came in to edit, he asked, "Where do we start?" I told him I would play his preferred take while rolling all four cameras at once. At the appropriate time, when he pointed to the monitor that represented the camera he wanted, I would cut to it. He said, "I find it very difficult to watch the four monitors at once." I had forgotten that film directors were used to a different way of editing. They mostly shot with a single camera, and *Faerie Tale Theatre* was shot on videotape with four or five cameras in sync. So I told him I would roll all the tapes and pick the shots myself. He could just watch the big monitor and let me know if he liked what he saw.

I started rolling the tapes and switching the cameras, and he shouted, "That's great! Keep doing what you're doing." We then played the switched scene and fixed any late camera cuts or changed any camera angles that he wanted changed. We watched it through one more time for any performance changes he wanted to make. After he picked the new performances, he said, "You make the changes, and I'll come back tomorrow with Shelley and the other producers to view it."

The next day James came in with Shelley Duvall and the producers to view the cut and to make any changes they wanted to make. The session went very well. What a pleasure it was to work with Shelley and that whole group of producers. I guess they were happy with the way the edit session went because, when we were done, Shelley and Fred went to Carole Ann and asked her if they could edit the rest of the shows at Astin/Zappia—with me as editor. Carole Ann told them we would be glad to accommodate them and assured Shelley that I would be their editor.

Shelley Duvall and Carole Ann became good friends, and Shelley's company loved the way Carole Ann and Lori handled their show from start to finish. I hadn't previously realized what happened to the clients and their show after I finished the editing. Carole Ann followed that show through every step to make sure nothing fell through the cracks. That girl may be even smarter than I thought she was.

How Shelley Duvall's show was handled and how her crew was treated made a big difference in whether they would come back to a facility to do their next project.

In addition, the show had two associate producers, Andy Copley and Sandra Pearson. They would alternate shows and follow the show through to sweetening, color correcting, and making copies for delivery to Showtime. They were very good at what they did. Also, I did several more *Tales* with Jim Frawley, with whom I was very comfortable. Some directors didn't like shooting or editing on videotape because they hadn't worked in the medium before and they were more comfortable with film.

Jim however adapted quite well to Videotape and the four-camera way of shooting.

As the editor, I felt it was my job to make the director and producers as comfortable as possible by guiding the session with great confidence. I explained the process whenever I felt they didn't understand what I was doing. I hope they walked away from the session with a little more understanding of the tape process. I certainly know I learned a lot more about the creative side of editing from these great directors.

Lori King booked several more shows, including: *Perry Como In The Holy Land* (for which we won an editing Emmy), *John Wayne: The Duke Lives On*, and another sitcom, *What's Happening!* We had to hire another editor, a vice president of sales; a sales executive, Richard Greenberg; and a company manager, Ron Silvera. Later Bob Belcher was hired as vice president.

One of the episodes of Shelly's *Faerie Tale* series was "Snow White and the Seven Dwarfs." During this time, Brenda S. Miller and I were cutting the Perry Como special with the director, Sterling Johnson. We were up against an airdate, so Carole Ann asked Shelly if she could assign the "Snow White" episode to another editor, explaining to her the situation. She also told her that I would be nearby, though, if she needed me.

I didn't realize that this editor didn't like to be given notes on his cut. He took it personally and wouldn't do them, especially if he didn't agree with them. He had a personality that wasn't very suitable for dealing with people. Shelley came to me several times, asking me if I could talk to him. I did, and he got better, but evidently he had his own way of doing things. I told Shelley that I would be done in a week, and then I would go over the show with her and make all the changes they wanted.

When Shelley's session with the editor I assigned to her was over, she came to me and said, "Please Marco, don't ever do that to me again." I assured her that I would be editing the rest of her shows. After I finished ed'ting the Como show, I worked with the producers of "Snow White" and went over the notes from Shelley and the director. They were all fairly simple to do, and I thought they were good notes that should have been done. After this experience, I realized I could assign this editor only to clients who could tolerate his personality. (Believe it or not, there were a few.)

A show or film can be cut many ways, none of which are wrong; they're only different. Your job is to make suggestions, but the final decision is the client's.

Over a period of five years, I cut thirty-three episodes for Shelley, which included her *Tall Tales and Legends* series. I don't want to be accused of name-dropping, but I was fortunate enough to work with such great talents as Var Johnson, Claude Rains, Carl Reiner, Lee Remick, James Ear Jones, Christopher Reeve, Liza Minnelli, Jeff Bridges, and Mick Jagger, among others. In addition, Shelley's *Tales* gave me the opportunity to work with some great directors such as Peter Medak, Gilbert Cates, Nicholas Meyer, Roger Vadim, Tim Burton, Jerry London, Christopher Guest, and James Frawley.

Shelley Duvall was one of nicest people I ever met in my business. One year, the show and I were nominated for an Ace Award. Shelley bought a large table at the awards ceremony. Carole Ann and I went to the ceremony, along with Shelley, Fred, and all the producers.

1983 ACE AWARDS

Shelley was going to present one of the awards, and she was really nervous. She said she hated talking in front of a crowd. She wanted to test a few opening jokes on us. We helped her pick a couple of the jokes, and she did really well. We didn't win any awards, but we really had a lot of fun.

In 1981, *Perry Como in the Holy Land* was nominated for an editing Emmy. Our daughter, Roxanne, was 16 and our son, Robert, was 12. We decided that they would probably enjoy going to the ceremonies with us.

ACADEMY OF TELEVISION ARTS & SCIENCES

SIXTH ANNUAL CREATIVE ARTS EMMY AWARDS

SATURDAY, SEPTEMBER 6, 1980
EXHIBITION BUILDING
The Pasadena Center

Cocktails at six o'clock
Dinner at seven
Awards Presentation at eight-thirty

Black Tie   Table No. __70__

CREATIVE ARTS EMMY AWARDS

The Pasadena Center

ADMIT ONE

The ceremony was held at the Bonaventure Hotel. It was quite an event. They served cocktails at 6:00 p.m., dinner at 7:00 p.m., and the ceremony began at 8:00 p.m. The presenters for the category of editing a musical variety show were Jerry Stiller and Anne Meara. When they announced, "The winners are Marco Zappia and Brenda S. Miller," I couldn't believe it. What a thrill it was to win with my wife and kids at the ceremony to see it happen.

PRESENTERS: ANNE MEARA AND JERRY STILLER

When we got home, the mood was jubilant. Robert was holding the Emmy and dancing all around while my wife was calling everyone she knew to tell them that I had won. All in all, it was a great night.

In previous years, many of the shows I worked on made script binders with the name of the show embossed on the cover as souvenirs for each member of the cast and crew. Over the years, to cut costs, it became more common to reserve the binders for cast only. Still, I had received thirty to forty binders since the first one I got on *All in the Family*, and I had shelves built above the editing console in the offline room to display them. Many of the clients would comment on the script binders, and they loved to see what shows were up there. Pretty soon they were asking me, "If I had a binder made for our show, would you put it on your shelf?" I always said, "Sure, I'd be honored." I got quite a few more binders after that.

John Astin was a real gentleman and great person to work with, but we were both on the creative side of the industry, not businessmen. At that time we had four partners. John Astin, Dave Moore both who were great to work with and Hugh Mcguire and Myself. Hugh didn't want to spend any money to improve the outdated equipment. We took the company from no clients to doing so much business that we had to hire five more people. We had five or six regular big-name clients. We also added another offline room and an audio sweetening room.

We had reached the point where we had to update the equipment to go any further. The other partners told Carole Ann that it wasn't right that I was the only partner who was being paid a salary. I would like to have been there during that conversation. I do know Carole Ann told them that I was the only partner generating revenue, that I brought in all the clients, and I was the only partner who was working sixty hours a week. She said, "This Company is just an investment or a tax write-off for you guys, but to us it's the way we make our living."

Needless to say, Carole Ann and I decided to leave Astin/Zappia. However, before we left, Carole Ann made some phone calls to help some of our people get jobs. Val, my brother, went to work for Compact Video as an engineer. He went on to become one of the best post-production engineers in the business.

Ron Silveira went work for Compact as a Vice President of sales and became an intricate part of Compact's success. Ron is one of the "Good Guys."

The five years I was at Astin/Zappia were a great experience. I gained some new clients: *The Dean Martin Show*, Shelley Duvall's *Faerie Tale Theatre*, and many more. I had convinced Carole Ann to come to work with me and, I have to say, we became quite a team in the business.

What I learned from this whole experience of being part owner of a facility was the difference between being an employer and an employee. I now know both sides of the coin. I'm not so quick to judge some of the decisions the owners have to make.

CHAPTER SIX

EDITING GOES TO MODERN VIDEO FILM

In 1984 there were a lot of post-production facilities where I could work. Between my editing ability and Carole Ann's talent for handling clients, we were fortunate enough to have built a reputation such that most facilities wanted to hire us as a team. One of the facilities that called us was Modern Video Film, a facility located in Hollywood Calif. Modern Video was owned by Moshe Barkat. We got to know him when he was a client of ours at Astin/Zappia. We decided to meet with him and talk. He told us that they didn't have an editing department—they mostly did film transfers—but he wanted to start an editing department, and he knew we would be perfect for the job. After Carole Ann did her usual negotiations, we went to work for him.

Carole Ann organized and set up the editing department at Modern Video. She designed new work orders for the clients because, at that time, they used maintenance repair forms for what little editing they did. She then called all our clients to let them know about our new work situation.

Meanwhile, I was meeting with Moshe to tell him what I needed. He took me into two empty rooms that he was going to turn into edit bays. One was slated to be an offline room and the other an online room, both controlled by CMX systems. I asked when the bays would be ready, and he said they'd be done when I needed them. That didn't make me feel very secure.

Moshe had one edit bay that was up and running with an old Sony editing system I knew nothing about. When I came in one morning, Moshe told me that he had a project he wanted me to work on with one of his clients. He said, "You can learn the system while you do the job; the client is in the room now." Lee Grey was assisting me, and thank God he was able to help me operate the system. The client must have thought, "So this is the famous Marco Zappia—he can't even make an edit without the help of his assistant." Thanks, Moshe!

Carole Ann called Moshe and me to her office to tell us that she had scheduled a new sitcom, *Who's the Boss?* As well as one of Shelly Duvall's *Faerie Tale Theatre* episodes, "The Princess and the Pea." She told Moshe we would need the edit bays up in about two weeks. He assured her that they would be ready.

After about a week, Moshe hadn't even started on the edit bays. Carole Ann, after booking a couple of more shows, made an edit schedule on a large piece of cardboard. She wrote on the top: "A picture is worth a thousand words. This is the schedule for the rooms that don't exist." She then placed the schedule on the empty chair in his office. When Moshe saw the schedule, he called her and, with his strong Israeli accent, he said, "Don't worry, Carole Ann, it'll get done!" Friday, on our way out the door as we passed Moshe's office, I said, "I still see two empty rooms." He yelled out, "See you Monday morning!"

That Monday morning when we came in to work, Moshe called us over and said, "I want to show you something." Moshe opened the door to one of the empty edit rooms. To our surprise, we were looking at a full-blown offline room. Moshe told us that the online room would be done by the following Monday. We were really relieved. Carole Ann could then start scheduling, and I had the rest of the week to test the room and have the maintenance crew fix any of the bugs. A couple of days later, I told Moshe that he had one hell of a maintenance crew headed by Al Hart. They put that room together over the weekend, and it worked. There were very few problems.

Al Hart was the head Engineer at MVF. He was a man of very few words but he excelled in designing any post production room we needed.

The following week, the *Who's The Boss?* Executive producers, Marty Cohen and Blake Hunter, came in with the director, Bill Persky, the associate producer, Ken Stump, and associate director, Gail Bergman. It was the usual crowd that comes in for a pilot. Whenever we had a new client, Carole Ann always made it a point to come in and introduce herself and let them know that she was there to help if they had any problems. She also had Moshe come in and introduce himself. With his round baby face, Moshe could charm the birds out of the trees. Clients were always impressed when the owner of the company took the time to come in and introduce himself.

Every time I started an edit session with a new group of producers, I was always a little nervous until I saw how they worked and had a chance to figure out their personalities. When they said, "Hi, Marco. Your reputation has preceded you," all I could say was "Don't believe anything you've heard about me until I finish cutting your first show." We all laughed and the edit session started off on a good note.

When starting with a new client group, let them discover how good you are by your work. This introductory time will give you a chance to learn how they work and their vision for the show. No matter how good you think you are, you can always learn more from each job you do.

Who's the Boss? Was another show that had a great ensemble of actors: Tony Danza, Judith Light, Katherine Helmond, Danny Pinaturo, and Alyssa Milano. This cast was an editor's dream. Their comedy timing was great. At that time, Alyssa Milano was about eight or nine, and I couldn't believe how good she was. Whether she was on camera or off, she was always in the scene. In my experience, often actors who weren't on camera would just stare into space waiting for their next line rather than reacting to the scene in progress. Not Alyssa; I could always count on her for the right reaction at any time. She was always present in the scene whether the camera was on her or not, and that's a gift to an editor.

Carole Ann made a lifelong friend in Jody Levin when she worked at Modern. Jody eventually left to go to work for Tri-Star Productions and was responsible for bringing us *My Two Dads*. The producer of *My Two Dads*, Michael Jacobs, told Jody that he already had an editor he liked, but she told him that because it was a Tri-Star project, he had to bring the pilot to Modern Video Film. Michael reluctantly agreed.

It was a great pilot—well written, great cast, well directed—I just knew it was going to sell and, sure enough, *My Two Dads* was on the air from 1987 to 1990. I did the cut with one of the producers, Mark Brull. He was a very knowledgeable guy, not only about editing but also about life. No matter on what subject you asked him a question, he could answer.

When Michael came in to view the cut, he introduced himself to me, and the viewing began without interruption. When it was over, he turned to me and said, "I'm very disappointed." When I asked why, he said, "After the first cut I usually spend a week in the editing room doing several more cuts, but with your cut I have only a few fixes before we send it to ABC for their notes.

Michael is a writer and producer whose work has appeared on Broadway, Off-Broadway, television, and film. His first play opened at the Biltmore Theatre in 1978 when he was twenty-two years old, making him one of the youngest playwrights in Broadway history. Over the next eighteen years, I was fortunate to work with Michael on eleven of his TV series.

Michael was a loyal client and a good friend after the *My Two Dads* pilot. He was one of the producers with whom I really enjoyed working. Like John Rich, Michael was one of those guys who, when he asked you to do something on your equipment, and you said it couldn't be done, he'd ask why not. Before you knew it, you figured out how to do it. I learned a lot from Michael about editing.

One of the things I learned from Michael was to pay attention to the small details of a performance. For instance, when you play the different performances of a particular line, and they are all equally good, the way to pick the best performance is to watch the actor's facial expression. Watch for emotion in his or her eyes, or lips, or a slight head movement. This practice also applies for a reaction shot.

On one episode of *My Two Dads*, Michael (played by Paul Reiser) and Joey (played by Gregg Evigan) didn't like the guy their daughter Nicole (played by Stacy Keenan) was dating. They grounded her and sent her to her room. That night, she snuck out of her bedroom window. When Joey went in to check on her and found her gone, he waited until she got back. A little later she climbed back through the window and crossed the room to turn on the lights. When she turned, she saw Joey standing at the window with his back to her. We cut back to Nicole saying "Dad," and cut back to Joey as he turned around to Nicole. She said, "I'm sorry" and we cut back to see him walk out of the room without saying a word. That was how the scene was written and shot.

My daughter was the same age as the Nicole character, and I knew there was a lot more emotion to be dug out of that scene. There were six or seven takes of the scene, so I watched them all to see if I could get an idea of how to cut it. I noticed in every take Nicole said her line a little differently and that Joey's non-reaction was a little different each time. Every time I cut to either Joey or Nicole, I would use a different take so it wouldn't look like I was repeating the same shot.

This is the way I cut the scene. After Nicole crossed the room to turn the lights on, she turned back and saw Joey. I cut to Joey at the window with his back to her, then back to Nicole saying "Dad," back to Joey still with his back to her, back to Nicole for "Dad" again, back to Joey as he turned around and stood silently, back to Nicole saying "I'm sorry," back to Joey for a moment, back to a silent shot of Nicole, and finally back to Joey's close-up cut wide as he crossed and walked out without saying a word. We faded out on a close-up of Nicole's face.

Remember, the editor's job is to inject heart and emotion into a scene.

The bedroom scene was the only one I cut without the producer sitting next to me. Mark Brull had to go back to the studio because they were starting to shoot again. If I had cut the scene the way it had been shot, the note from Michael would have been, "Something is wrong with that scene. You know what to do—fix it." I sent the cut to Michael's office with a note saying, "I finished the cut so that you wouldn't have to wait another day to view it."

Later that day I got a call from Michael, and he said, "I have a lot of notes on the show, but don't let anyone tell you to change one frame of that scene in the bedroom! I watched it several times, and each time it got to me."

The reason I tell you this story is to remind you to look at every frame of the footage that was shot. You never know what you will need to cut a scene. If you feel something isn't working in the scene, go with your gut, look at the footage, and something will come to you.

Carole Ann had to have surgery and stay home a couple of weeks. When Michael heard about it, he came down to my edit room and said, "If you and Carole Ann need anything, let me know. I could send my whole office staff to clean your house, wait on her, and make her meals." I told him that I appreciated the offer, but she already had good help. He then said, "I mean it. If you need anything, just call me."

Carole Ann was really touched by the offer. Michael and the staff sent her the most gorgeous flowers from Mark's Garden we had ever seen. Michael always came through for us in business and in friendship. He has a great heart!

After a while we got so busy that Modern Video Film had to build more editing rooms. We hired two more editors: Larry Harris and Michael Sachs. They had some pretty big clients of their own that they brought over with them. They met with Carole Ann about scheduling these clients, and she asked them what made them come to work for Modern. They said, "We heard how fast Modern is growing and how well the clients are being treated, and we wanted to work for that kind of facility."

Being married to an editor, Carole Ann understood how tough those long hours were on the family. She always tried to schedule the editors, whenever possible, to get home for family events. They loved the way she treated them and their clients, and the way she handled their shows.

One day I was in my offline room editing *Who's the Boss?* With the assistant director, Gail Bergman, when my old mentor, director John Rich, walked into the room with three three-quarter cassettes. He dropped them on my console and said, "You've got to fix these shows." I said, "John, I'm in a session. What are these?"

He told me that the cassettes contained three episodes of *MacGyver*, and I had to do him a favor: watch the tapes and fix them. He wanted the shows ready for viewing the next afternoon at Paramount Studios. John was not only my mentor; he was also an old friend, so I felt I owed him the effort.

When my *Who's the Boss?* Session ended, I watched the three episodes of *MacGyver*. I decided that they were good cuts; all they needed was better pacing. So using the tapes John brought as playback, I took the shows down a generation and tightened where I felt it was needed. I also got rid of any reactions that slowed down the show.

The first cut is your cut. It's your chance to show your creativity and show the producers a cut that is close to what they want. A lot of times an editor will do a cut that is loosely paced thinking that the producers should have a chance to give their notes before the editor tightens and paces the show. Not true! Use your instincts and pace the show the way you think it should be paced. If the producers could spend more time doing their jobs instead of being in the edit room doing yours, they'd be much happier.

I took the cuts to Paramount the next day thinking I was going to play them for John only; instead he lead me into a conference room filled with Paramount executives. John's partner, actor-turned-producer Henry Winkler, was also there. Everyone watched the three tapes, and they were thrilled with the results. Henry said, "You have to do a cut on all our shows." I told him I was cutting four shows, so I didn't have the time. All I could do was offer some advice. I said, "Your editors are good editors, but they were used to film, not the hectic pace of television editing on tape. So they made their first cut "loose" because on film it was a lot easier to cut a few frames than it was to add frames back."

A week later John came back to my edit bay and said, "I can't make airdates because the editors are taking too long to cut the show." So I took him to Carole Ann's office. John told her his problem and that he needed my help. I told Carole Ann and John that I had never cut an hour-long, single-camera action show before, and maybe that's just how long it takes.

Carole Ann said, "I guess you won't be able to say you've never cut a single-camera, hour-long show anymore." (She had a soft spot in her heart for John because of our history, so she wanted me to help him.) I said, "Besides not having ever cut that type of show, they're using some kind of nonlinear editing system that I don't know anything about." She countered, "You learn fast. Just cut one episode and see what's going on." I could never put one over on her.

Actually, I was looking forward to learning a nonlinear edit system, and I'd always wondered how cutting a single-camera show compared with cutting a multi-cam show. This was my chance to do both, so I paid *the MacGyver* show a visit. The production was using the Montage III digital editing system. This was the first videotape-based nonlinear system that utilized up to seventeen super beta hi-fi VCRs to offer random access to the material by recording all the same material on all seventeen-beta machines.

Nonlinear editing is a method that allows you to access any frame in a digital video clip regardless of sequence in the clip. The freedom to access any frame, and use a cut-and-paste method similar to the ease of cutting and pasting text in a word processor, allows you to easily include fades, transitions, and other effects that can't be achieved with linear editing.

Even though this was the first nonlinear system I had used, it wasn't the first nonlinear system to be introduced. The first system was introduced in 1961 by CMX; it was called the CMX 600. This was a joint venture between Memorex and CBS. It recorded and played back analog video on modified disk pack drives the size of washing machines. In the '80s, an approximation of a nonlinear, computer-based system was Lucas Film's Edit Droid, which used several laser discs of the same raw footage to simulate random access editing.

The Montage III had a time line, a digital representation of the footage that showed the layers of audio and video tracks, as well as a row of small monitors to display the first frame of each daily or the first and last frame of the edit. There was a wide screen master display in the middle.

An editor was assigned to train me on the Montage, and after I sat with him for about fifteen minutes, I knew that this was a great system. I told him all I needed was the time to play with the system on my own for a while, and I'd be ready to edit the next *MacGyver* episode. Every chance I got I would learn more about what the Montage could do.

Once again I'll remind you to learn the edit system to the point where you don't even have to think about it. You then can concentrate on your editing.

It took seven days to shoot an episode of *MacGyver*, which was a one-hour show. There were three editors on staff, and they each edited every third episode. After the director finished shooting for the day, the "dailies," (the day's footage) were transferred to tape. The next day the tapes were delivered to us along with the script pages. Our assistants transferred dailies to the Montage later that afternoon. That evening, after I finished editing my other shows, I would view the dailies. Only forty-five minutes to an hour's worth of dailies were shot each day.

Every editor has a different way of editing. Because the Montage was a nonlinear system, I could view all the dailies of a particular scene. I then marked my script pages, picking the takes I would use and mapping out some kind of cutting pattern. I built a rough cut, going with my first instincts. This gave me an idea what the scene looked like when it was assembled.

You could spend a lot of time on one edit only to find, when you saw the whole scene put together, it didn't mesh.

I watched the scene the way I had just built it, changed any shots that I thought didn't work, fixed the pacing, and changed any performances that didn't seem right. I worked on MacGyver from twelve midnight to four am. I then came in at nine am the next day to do my other shows. I loved every minute of it.

When I came in around Midnight the next day to edit MacGyver, I watched the scenes that I had edited the night before. When I saw them with fresh eyes, I was able to fix anything that I had missed. This took me about forty minutes. Then I started on the new dailies. I was able to keep up with filming, and, after I got my last day's dailies cut, I had a whole day to view the episode and correct anything I thought needed fixing. The next day I invited the director in to see the cut. After the director watched the cut, we did his fixes, which didn't take more than a couple of hours with the nonlinear system. The following day the producers came in, and I did their fixes, too. Next, the episode went to the network executives for their notes. Finally, we cut the show down to time before sending it to online and sweetening.

I couldn't believe how easy it was to edit a single-camera show with the Montage system. Putting a cut together was as easy as using a word processor. The time code was nonexistent because your cut was the edit list. All you had to do was to concentrate on the footage and let the creativity flow.

I then knew that post-production of an episode could be completed in eleven to twelve days compared to the seventeen or eighteen days it was now being done. Whenever I had a chance, I got to know the other editors and observed how they worked. There were two regulars: Howard Deane (who had edited such TV projects as *Colombo*, the *Nancy Drew* mysteries, the autobiography of G. Gordon Liddy, and many more) and Larry L. Mills, who had edited *M*A*S*H* for several years.

These guys were really good editors, but as I observed them I realized that they were still thinking about editing in terms of the old Moviola system, where the film editor had to carefully consider the cut as a whole before committing to making the splice. When you edited on a Moviola system, you were literally cutting out pieces of film with a razor and, if you changed your mind, putting back the pieces was laborious.

Even though Howard and Larry were working on the Montage, they would preview the cut several times, changing it only a frame or two at a time. I pointed out to them that, even though the show was shot on film, they had the advantage of editing on a nonlinear digital tape system. They didn't have to think in Moviola mode anymore. They could try anything easily (tighten or loosen cuts, change shots, change performances) and review the cut immediately, then try something else if they changed their minds. The show should be completed in eleven days instead of the seventeen or eighteen days it was taking.

I also explained to them how John liked to work, because if you know what the producers like, you're way ahead of the game. First of all, John liked the first cut to be paced as fast as possible. Also, when you make an edit, be ready to defend it. For instance, if John were to ask why you added a close-up at a certain point, explain why. He'll either agree with you, or tell you he doesn't like it, and so you change it. But if you say, "I don't know why I put the close-up in," he'll come in for the kill. John thinks that you as the editor should have a reason for making any edit, whether he agrees or not.

The biggest problem I had with the Montage system was that every time I went back to my regular edit bay and the linear system, I felt as if somebody sent me back a couple of hundred years.

Howard and Larry were good guys and good editors, and they had the right attitude. They appreciated my input, and we became good friends. I finished out the season with *MacGyver* by cutting a few more episodes. I used Howard and Larry on a couple of other shows that we also cut on the Montage: *Dinosaurs* and *Vietnam War Stories*.

John still called me whenever he had a problem with a particular editor, and I would meet with him and the editor to help work it out. After a couple of seasons, the producers moved the *MacGyver* show to Canada, and I wasn't involved with the show anymore.

One day, Gail Bergman, the AD on *Who's The Boss?* asked me if I could edit Tony Danza and Tracy Robinson's wedding for him. I said, "I'd be glad to do it." A few days later Tony and Tracy came to the edit bay, and we got started. Tony is a down-to-earth kind of guy with a great sense of humor, and Tracy is a refined, beautiful woman who also had a great sense of humor. Carole Ann came to the edit bay and introduced herself, and then she joined us. Tony would point to the screen and say "That's Uncle Nick. He's one of my relatives." and that's Rocco, one of my relatives."

I finally said, "Tony, I know your relatives because they all look like my relatives—a bunch of Brooklyn hoods."

We all laughed, and Carole Ann asked, "Tracy, which of your relatives do you want in?" Tony just laughed and said, "Yeah, we could put some of your relatives in, too." Between my wife and Tracy, Tony didn't have a chance. He was a good sport, and we had a great time; the rest of the session went really well.

One of Shelley's Duvall's *Tall Tales and Legends* series episodes that I edited was "Johnny Appleseed." Christopher Guest directed that particular episode. It was great working with him; it seemed as if he enjoyed the process, and this made the session fun.

Christopher wears many hats: director, actor, writer, comedian, singer and songwriter.

One-day Christopher's wife, Jamie Lee Curtis, came in to visit him. When it got around the building that Jamie was in my edit bay, all of a sudden I had more visitors than I had had in a month. The guys were a little disappointed because she came in wearing a sweatshirt and sweat pants. No matter what she was wearing, it was a real pleasure meeting her. Twelve years later, my son Robert worked with her when he wrote the story and screenplay for *Halloween: H2O*. Robert said that working with Jamie was a great experience.

I also worked with director Roger Vadim on one of Shelley's Duvall's *Faerie Tale Theatre* episodes— "Beauty and The Beast. Roger was first known for the movie, <u>And God Created Women</u>, which gave Brigitte Bardot international fame. Roger had done some episodic TV before but all on film. He seemed to be intrigued with videotape, and he was open to the whole editing process.

In 1988 Carole Ann got a call from Ron Silviera who had gone to work for Compact Video after leaving Astin/ Zappia. He said, "I heard that your contract is up with Modern Video Film. John Donlon, the CEO, wants to have lunch with you and Marco to talk about coming to work for Compact." We figured, why not? If nothing else, we'd get a free lunch. It didn't make much difference where we worked because our clients would follow us wherever we went as long as the place had the latest equipment, decent edit bays, and Carole Ann there to handle all the shows.

The next day we went to Compact Video's editing facility in beautiful downtown Burbank to take a tour. The rooms were very nice even though they had that '70s hot tub wood paneling. I knew the equipment was working because Compact was the facility where my brother Val went to work after we left Astin/Zappia.

I always felt secure with the equipment when I knew Val was in charge of keeping everything running smoothly. We noticed that, as nice as the facility was, the four-offline bays and five out of the six online bays were empty, and this was at the peak of the TV season.

We then went to lunch at the Smokehouse (which has excellent garlic bread). As we sat at our table, John started telling me why I should go to work for Compact. He kept all his comments directed at me. When he was finished, I said, "You're talking to the wrong person." I pointed to Carole Ann and added, "She handles all my negotiations. Also, I'll tell you this much, John, if we end up working for Compact Video, you'll have a great opportunity to hire some of the top editors in the industry. They'll follow Carole Ann wherever she goes. They know that she'll look after them and their clients." The look on John's face was priceless when he realized he had been completely ignoring her.

He then turned to Carole Ann and gave his whole pitch all over again. John said he would throw in a car. I spoke up and said, "Great! I always wanted a new pickup truck." Carole Ann turned to me, put her hand on my shoulder and said, "Honey, I'll buy you a truck for Christmas. John, you get him a Jaguar." And that's the way it happened.

Negotiating for yourself is a real art, and if you can't do it yourself, get someone who can. If it happens to be your wife, whom you know is on your side, better yet. My parents didn't raise a fool for a son.

We gave Modern Video Film two weeks notice. When we started at MVF , they had one editing room. When we left, they had twelve edit bays and had gone from no editing income to eleven million a year. Also the revenue grew in every department, Telecine, Audio, Dubs and so on. So I feel we did what we told Moshe we would do.

CHAPTER SEVEN

NEW CLIENTS AND NEW EXPERIENCES

I n 1988 we went to work for Compact Video. Editing technology hadn't changed much for a while, so the work at Compact Video wasn't that different from what I was used to doing. Most editors were still doing offline cuts on three-quarter tapes with a CMX or a Mach One system. Compact Video had all the rooms equipped with the Mach One system, which I preferred. I found it to be user-friendly, and I liked working with an active edit list. During the five years I was at Compact, I edited *Faerie Tale Theater*, *Boy Meets World*, *Roseanne*, *Dinosaurs* (an animatronics show created by Michael Jacobs), *Singer and Sons*, *My Two Dads*, *Home Improvement* and *Who's The Boss?*

Carole Ann and I were a great team. There were times when she would call me in my edit bay to tell me that John, the CEO, was in her office, and ask me to come in to say hello. I knew she did this because she was trying to get something done for a client, so I'd ask her on the phone if I were mad or happy. If she said mad, when I got into her office I would say "Hi" to John, and then something like, "I want to know why it's taking so long to take care of this problem, John. My clients are very upset; this has to be taken care of right away!

If Carole Ann had told me I was happy, I would say, "Thanks, John, for taking care of the problem. I really appreciate it." Later on I'd ask Carole Ann what the situation was all about and she'd tell me. It worked well for us.

One of the first new shows I did at Compact was *Roseanne.* Carole Ann got a call from Gayle Maffeo, one of the producers of the show. Gayle and I had worked together way back in the CBS days. She told Carole Ann that she thought I was the perfect guy to work with Matt Williams, the creator and producer of the show. They had already shot the pilot, and Gayle wanted us to meet with Matt.

For several years Matt Williams supported himself as an actor, performing on stage and television and doing voiceovers while writing plays. Matt then joined the Cosby show during its premiere season and worked as a writer/ producer on the show for three years. Williams' subsequent success with A Different World and Roseanne led to the establishment of Wind Dancer in 1989 with partners David McFadzean and Carmen Finestra.

The next day we met in Matt's office and watched the pilot. I asked Matt if he wanted the series to be edited the way the pilot was, and he said not necessarily. I told him that I thought the pilot was not paced right, and Roseanne seemed to go out of character when she laughed at her own joke. He said if I could improve on it, he would be glad to see it.

The way I cut the show was such that when Roseanne said something funny to the kids, I would cut to one of the kid's reactions, and then back to Roseanne's laugh, then back to the kids. That made Roseanne's laugh more of an "I gotcha" laugh rather than a laugh at her own joke.

On one episode they did a scene in the kitchen followed by a scene in the living room and then back to the kitchen. Matt wanted to eliminate the living room scene without a dissolve to make it as if the two kitchen scenes were a continuous action. The dialogue cut together in the script, but I had to figure how to make it work visually.

I didn't know how I was going to merge the two kitchen scenes, so I watched all the footage in that area. I ran across a take where, after the first living room scene ended, Roseanne got up off the couch and walked into the kitchen. The tape was still rolling even though the director had yelled, "Cut." So I used that visual; the last thing we saw in the first kitchen scene was Jackie talking after Roseanne had walked out of frame. When we put the two-kitchen scenes together, I used the footage of the back of Roseanne walking toward Jackie. I played a couple of words from Roseanne's line over the back of her head and then cut to her face just as she arrived in front of Jackie. It was seamless.

I always say for the times you can't be good, you have to be lucky.

The Directors Guild of America (DGA) requires that a guild member be in the room while the editor is cutting an episode, but producer Gayle Maffeo told me she didn't think I needed an AD looking over my shoulder, so she got me into the DGA, which was a big break for me.

The director of the first seven episodes was Ellen Falcon. She shot seven or eight takes of every scene. This meant I had to look at every take and pick the performances. Because of my training with John Rich, this process did not take very long. I would cut the show in about a day and a half and send it off to the director to view. She did not have many notes, but, after a couple of episodes, she called me and asked, "How could you cut the show so fast and still have watched all the takes?" I told her it was just easy for me, and then I asked her if there was anything wrong with the cuts. She told me she loved the cuts, but she wanted to make sure that I was picking the best performances.

On the next episode, Ellen wanted to sit with me and pick the performances herself. I played all the takes of each performance for her. After a couple of script pages of material she asked me, "Which one would you pick?" I picked the take, and I told her why. She then said, "You can do this without me. Keep doing what you do."

Michael Jacobs brought a pilot in for me to edit. The show was *Boy Meets World*. From all my years of editing, I knew that every once in a while you get a show that has a perfect cast—this show was one of them. The cast was Ben Savage, Rider Strong, Danielle Fishel, Will Friedle, William Daniels, Betsy Randle and William Russ. Ben Savage's comedic timing was perfect. Every time I did a pilot for Michael, he would ask me if I thought it would sell. I would not lie to a client, so I told Michael that not only was this show going to sell, but also it would be on the air for several years. As it turned out, *Boy Meets World* ran for seven years.

When I did another pilot for Michael, *Almost Home,* he asked me what I thought. Before I could answer, one of the producers said to him, "Why bother asking him? He'll only tell you what you want to hear." That's when Michael said, "Marco has always told me the truth, and he has always been right."

I told Michael that *Almost Home* was a good, sweet show, but it would probably be on the air only about two seasons because the network wouldn't give it a chance. NBC aired thirty-three episodes before it cancelled the show.

Today I could never be that accurate. The network people are not that savvy. It's all about the money, not about the creative side. If the network owns the show, it will keep the show on the air a lot longer to give it a chance to be what they call a hit.

In 1991 Gayle Maffeo brought in another pilot created by Matt Williams, Carmen Fiestra, and David MacFadzean. It was called *Home Improvement.* This was another show with a great cast. It was a sitcom based on Tim Allen's stand-up routine. John Pasquin directed the first thirty-eight episodes.

As it happened, Gayle brought my son Robert to meet Matt. He started as a show runner. He was then moved up to writer's assistant. and he worked their for about eight years. When I was working with Gayle at CBS, she was pregnant with her daughter at the same time Carole Ann was pregnant with Robert. Who would have known that twenty-one years later Robert would be working with Gayle?

One day Matt Williams saw Robert writing something at his desk and asked him, "What are you writing?" Robert told him that it was a short comedy. Matt read it and told him to go home and rewrite it without the jokes. Matt's point was that he was writing to the joke rather than let-ting the character and the situation create the humor. Matt took it upon himself to become Robert's mentor, and Robert eventually worked his way up to staff writer.

I worked with Nicholas Meyer when he directed, "The Pied Piper of Hamlin," one of the episodes of the *Faerie Tale Theatre* series. Nicholas was first known for his best-selling novel, *The Seven Percent* Solution, a 1974 Sherlock Holmes novel. He was also known for directing the films, *Time After Time*, two of the Star Trek motion pictures, and the TV movie *The Day After*.

Andy Copely was the associate producer of this episode, and she sat with us in the edit bay. All through the editing process, I kept mistakenly referring to the character of the mayor of Hamlin as the king, and Nicholas would always correct me. Now in my defense, as weak as it may be, the character wore a robe that I thought only a king would wear. After about five days of my calling the mayor the king, Nicolas finally got fed up and said, "Marco, you may be a good editor, but you've got a mind like a sieve." We laughed because it was true—I just couldn't get it straight. Andy got mad at him for saying that, but I told her that he was right; after a few days I was getting mad at myself. From then on the session went very well.

I worked with Peter Medak on four *Faerie Tales*: "The Snow Queen," "Pinocchio," "The Emperor's New Clothes," and "The Dancing Princesses." Peter's more notable movies are: *Ruling Class*, *The Changeling*, and *Zorro the Gay Blade*.

The first shot of a scene Peter always liked doing wide shots that slowly pushed to a close up. Shelley wanted to go in closer sooner, but like most directors, when Peter wanted to protect his shot choices, he didn't shoot any alternate coverage. Peter was really a good director. I liked the way he shot the episodes because he used a lot of tracking shots and crane shots.

During the editing of "The Emperor's New Clothes," the bathroom upstairs leaked and poured into our edit bay from the ceiling. Water got all over Peter's new coat that was hanging over the back of his chair. Peter was a great sport about it. Carole Ann had his coat sent to a good dry cleaner, shut down the session for the day, and took Peter out to lunch.

Because I was doing so many shows at one time for Disney Studios (*Home improvement*, *Boy Meets World*, *Lost at Home*, *Soul Man*, and *Thunder Alley*), the executives there wanted me to do the editing on the lot where I would be more accessible to the producers and directors. So Compact Video had Val put together an offline editing system that was installed for me on the Disney lot in Burbank in the film editing building. We set up a Mach One editing system that ran five three-quarter inch Sony Umatic tape machines. Disney had to install a five-ton air conditioning unit on the roof to feed just that one room to keep all the needed equipment cool.

With this arrangement, instead of driving across town to see their cuts, the producers could just walk across the lot to my edit bay. I had boxes of three-quarter inch tapes lined up in the hallway for all the shows I was editing, as well as two or three episodes of each show. Up until this point the editor onlined his own shows but, because I was editing so many shows at once, other editors would on-line the shows for me, and I shared the editing credits with them.

In 1991 Michael Jacobs called Carole Ann to book another show with me. The show was a sitcom with a pretty standard structure except that it portrayed a family of dinosaurs and their strange lifestyle. The name of the show was *Dinosaurs*, and the characters were all created with animatronics. The show was shot on film with one, or sometimes two, cameras. The director shot several takes to get all the angles needed to make it look like a regular sitcom family.

With this project, I was glad to see that I was re-introduced to the Montage III edit system. Although the Walt Disney Company produced *Dinosaurs*, we cut the show in a rented space on the CBS Bradford lot in Studio City. This is also where *Dinosaurs* was filmed. We hired Howard Deane and Larry Mills, with whom I had worked on *MacGyver*, to be the second and third editors. Before my show came up to edit, the Disney executives wanted to have a meeting in executive producer Michael Jacobs' office with me, Carole Ann, producer Mark Brull, a half dozen Disney people, and Michael, of course. Carole Ann and I had no idea what the meeting was about, but Mark Brull knew, and he warned Michael Jacobs ahead of time.

When we entered the room, Michael shook my hand and gave Carole Ann a hug. He then went back to his chair, sat down, leaned back, and placed both feet on the desk. He asked the Disney executives, "Why are we here?"

One of the Disney guys spoke up and said, "Marco is doing so many shows, we don't think he'll have time to edit *Dinosaurs*. Michael told them that no matter how many shows I was doing at once, I never missed an airdate. So the Disney guy added, "Because it's a film show, we don't think Marco will be able to cut it. Cutting single-camera film is a lot different than cutting tape. We need a creative editor on the show because editing film takes a lot more skill." Was I insulted? No, I was taught to always consider the "source." Enough said?

Michael then took his feet off of his desk, slowly leaned forward and said, "If this meeting is about whether Marco is going to edit this show, this meeting is over. I have been on the phone all day long with ABC talking about what directors are going to direct *Dinosaurs*, but the truth is I don't care who directs as long as Marco Zappia is the editor. I would put his first cut on the air without even watching it ahead of time; that's how much faith I have in his ability to cut this show."

Michael stood up, walked over to Carole Ann, gave her a kiss on the cheek and in a voice loud enough for the Disney people to hear, he said to her, "If they give you any trouble, call me." Needless to say, Disney wasn't exactly in love with us after that.

The first episode of *Dinosaurs* I was scheduled to edit had a four-minute outdoor scene with the dinosaurs in a forest. It took two days to shoot that one scene. There was a lot of material to look through—about three hours. I felt the only way to edit a scene with so much footage was to view every frame. First I viewed all takes of the wide shots and marked in the script where I thought I could use certain takes. I did the same with all of the different angles that were shot. I was going back to the days when we had to make a paper edit list. After I spent four hours viewing the footage and making my paper edit list, I started building my rough cut of the scene. This step took me about an hour and a half.

I was just getting ready to watch the scene to see if the cut made any sense when Michael walked into the edit room and introduced me to Dean Valentine, who at that time was the president of ABC programming. He said that he had brought Mr. Valentine in to show him some footage so that he could see how *Dinosaurs* looked on the screen. I told him that I had just built the outdoor scene, but it was very rough. Michael said, "That's OK, we just want to see how the footage looks."

After I played the scene, they thanked me, and as they started to leave, Michael stopped and said, "By the way, if I saw that scene in the show I would probably have only one or two small notes. Good job."

Normally, *after I view all the footage, I like to bang through a cut of the scene without looking back until I finish. Then I go back and watch the scene through. You'd be surprised how well it turns out. It's like typing a letter on a word processor. If you just bang out the letter and don't stop until you've finished, then go back and look at it, you'll find something you might've changed flows nicely when you see it in the completed letter.*

Another incident happened while editing *Dinosaurs*. Michael and Mitch Banks, one of the producers, came in to view the director's cut of the show. As I usually do, I had the script ready to write down Michael's notes. All through the show Michael said, "that's not right" or "that's not how the scene should look." Then after the viewing, instead of giving me specifics, Michael stood up and said, "Marco, fix it, you know what to do," and left the room. Mitch then came to me and said, "Michael didn't give you any notes; how do you know what to do?" I told him Michael had given me all the notes I needed to know what he wanted done—his verbal cues were enough.

If you learn how the producer's creative thought process works, it'll be a big advantage to getting the first cut as close as possible to what he or she wants.

One of the *Faerie Tale Theatre* shows I did was "Aladdin and His Wonderful Lamp." On the day we started editing, this strange man with a lot of energy and quirky hair walked in and introduced himself: episode director, Tim Burton. Editing with Tim was a great experience. Tim's version of this classic was different and hilarious. Tim had James Earl Jones (The Genie) and Leonard Nimoy (the Magician) play their characters very campy, and they had a lot fun with it. Tim Burton definitely put his own stamp on this classic.

One day, Tim had to leave the edit bay in the middle of the day for a directing job interview on Pee-wee Herman's first movie. We all waited for him to get back to tell us what happened. Finally he walked into the room and said, "I got it!" Since then, look what a great director he has become.

CHAPTER EIGHT

NEW TECHNOLOGY AT MODERN VIDEO FILM

I n 1993 our contract was up with Compact Video, so Carole Ann and I went to work for Modern Video Film again. We kept our existing editing room on the Disney lot, and Modern rented the equipment from Compact. Since we had last worked for Modern, they had moved from Hollywood to Burbank. Nothing changed for me, but Carole Ann once again had to do all the work. She set up a new office at Modern and notified all the clients. Editors Larry Harris and Michael Sachs, as well as all their clients, followed us to Modern. I was editing *Boy Meets World*, *Home Improvement*, and *Dinosaurs*. Soon I picked up two more shows, *Thunder Alley* for Matt Williams and *Where I Live*, for Michael Jacobs.

In 1994 I heard about the Avid nonlinear editing system from Jeff Bass, one of the editors at Modern who was also a computer genius. I asked him to have them set up one of the systems on the DISNEY lot, and I would play with it when I had a chance, then let them know what I thought of it. The only nonlinear system I had used up till then was the Montage 3 for single-camera shows, and I had loved that system.

When I tested the Avid system, after just fifteen minutes I thought, "Wow! This is the future nonlinear editing system for television." The only problem was that Avid wasn't ready yet for editing multi-camera shows. I asked Jeff to see if we could keep the Avid on the lot for the rest of the season with the idea of teaming up with Avid's programmers to make the system work for multi-camera shows. Moshe, the head of Modern, agreed to let Jeff work with me on the lot whenever I needed him. Because I wasn't that familiar with Avid, I had Jeff learn how to operate it first, so he would be able to teach me how to use it. We had the studio give us a quad split feed, a separate tape that shows footage from all four different angles simultaneously, along with the four individual camera tapes.

I still edited my shows on the Mach One linear system, but I also had Jeff input all the material into the Avid system so we could work with the Avid engineers. I loved the random access of the footage Avid offered, but not being able to roll the four cameras in sync and switch to any camera at a given time by just pressing a button was a real drawback.

Jeff and I had worked together for a long time, so he knew how I worked. I would tell Jeff what features I wanted, and he'd work with the Avid techs to deliver them. Then I would test the changes and have them fix any problems. My theory was that the fewer keystrokes you had to hit to make a function happen, the better. For example, to turn on all the audio and video tracks, you had to hit a button for each track. So I asked Jeff to find out if there was a macro feature that would allow me to turn on all tracks with one keystroke. Being an Avid testing site for the Avid was great because it allowed me to give input on how the multi-cam and other features were developed. Working with Jeff was a real lifesaver.

Jeff and I worked with the Avid system until the end of the TV production season then went to Avid to talk about the future. Since the multi-cam feature wasn't fully developed, we asked if the company would put three Avid edit systems and two digitizing stations on the lot for next season. I said, "I'll be editing three of my top-rated shows on the Avid: *Who's The Boss*, *Home Improvement*, and *Boy Meets World*. We would continue to be their beta site, and since we would be the first to use their system to edit four- camera sitcoms, Avid could use us to promote their products. They agreed and delivered the equipment.

Jeff and I went to Disney and explained to the executives the arrangement we had made with Avid and how it would benefit them. That is, the Avid system would take fewer hours to cut an episode, which meant we'd be able to deliver a show much faster. But it was a hard sell because, even though Disney wasn't paying for any of the equipment, the studio had to give up the real estate to house the equipment. Finally we convinced them. They couldn't give us the space we needed in one building, so the systems were spread all around the Burbank lot.

During the off-season, Jeff and I made a list of things we would like the Avid to do. By the beginning of the next production season, we had the macro feature, a version of the multi-cam, and we asked for and got a "virtual reel," which allowed us to "multi-group" or sync-lock all the performances from all the cameras on one virtual reel. That saved us the manual labor of going through the script and naming and organizing the different takes.

During the season, with our input, Avid continued to improve the multi-cam feature as well as many other functions. Another great feature of a nonlinear system is that you no longer had to deal with an edit list. No more dealing with time code. Your cut is your edit list.

During the next production season, we cut a lot of shows on the Avid as we continued testing the system. Cutting three shows with airdates was tough because there were a lot of bugs in each new update on the Avid's hardware and software that the engineers sent to test. With Jeff working mostly on the Avid changes; I had Disney hire Keith Gore as my second assistant. In those days most of the changes were hardware driven. Today. with a good computer like a Mac dual 2.3 GHz power PC G5 with 2 GB DDR2 SDRAM of memory, all you have to do is keep updating the software, and you're up to speed.

In 1995, our Avid test year was up. We asked the Disney executives if they were interested in buying the systems, but they told us they didn't want to own any equipment. Modern didn't want to buy the systems either. So Carole Ann and I partnered with Jeff Bass and bought all the Avid equipment, which we subsequently rented back to Disney.

Disney had a free ride and didn't have to pay for any of the equipment, including the drives for the previous year. I relied on Carole Ann to negotiate the purchase price of the equipment and the credit financing terms, as well as the rate Disney would pay for the rental. As usual the negotiations went very well on both issues. I have to tell you this is a woman you want on your side of the table for any negations.

Eventually Disney constructed a building that housed Windancer, the company that produced *Home Improvement*. We had five rooms in the back of the building for all of our equipment. With the two digitizing stations and the three editing systems in one building, and all the material stored on removable nine gigabyte drives, all I had to do was go from room to room, do my editing, then turn the cut over to one of my assistants to output it or back up the show and get the system ready for the next project.

The development of the Avid nonlinear editing system (and having it housed right there on the lot) made it much easier to get the producers to come to the editing bay and view the cut. Before, I would send the cut to their offices where they would view it, then send it back to me to try some changes. I'd send it back with notes on which changes worked and which didn't. This back and forth meant making several passes OF the cut.

With the Avid system, I could access all the footage, make changes, and show them to producers right away. They could decide right then and there in the edit bay if the changes were working or not; the show then went to the network. After the network changes, the show went to the online bay. We made a lot fewer cuts as a result.

Soon I was cutting five Disney shows at one time: *Boy Meets World*, *Maybe This Time* and *Misery Loves Company* produced by Michael Jacobs, and *Home Improvement* and *Buddies* produced by Matt Williams, Carmen Finestra and David MacFadzean at Windancer Production. So I hired another assistant, Kevin Mullich, to work the night shift and input the material that was shot each day. Kevin turned out to be a real asset to the editing team. When I was doing only one or two shows Kevin stayed on to assist me. Not only was he a great assistant editor, but also he was a good technician. He built all my dubbing racks and kept the equipment running.

I could never cut that many shows at one time without a great team of assistants to back me up.

Both Michael Jacobs and the Windancer guys were very understanding about my situation, and they worked around my schedule. However, I always made sure I got the first cut done the day after the shoot.

One day a columnist from the Hollywood Reporter called me and wanted to know if she could do an interview with me. She said that in a couple of weeks the publication was going to dedicate one whole edition to all the crafts, and someone had suggested that she talk to me about editing. She said she knew that I edited all genres, and she wanted to know how I prepared myself when I had to go from editing comedy to drama. I wasn't sure exactly what she was asking, so I told her, "As I watch all the footage, I pick performances. Then I edit."

She then said, "No, I mean how do you psych yourself up to go from genre to genre."

I told her that no matter what genre I was working with it was the same, "I watch all the footage, and then I edit."

After she asked the question several more times, and I gave the same answer, I finally said, "The way I see it, whether you're cutting a comedy, drama, or action, editing any scene is the same. The director, the actors, and the script tell you how to cut the scene. When you're watching the footage, watch how the director shoots the scene, watch the actor's performance, and know the story that the script is telling you. Keeping all these things in mind after you watch the footage, the scene will practically cut itself." I guess she wanted some big psychological answer because, needless to say, she never included me in the article.

That interview reminds me of the times when my daughter would come home from school and ask me to help with her math problems. She had the hardest time with the thought problems. You know the kind, where a train is traveling sixty miles an hour for the first twenty miles and forty miles per hour for the next sixty miles, etc., etc. When I read the problem I knew the answer before I finished reading it. My daughter would say, "OK, that's the answer, but how did you solve it?" I would tell her I didn't know; that the answer just came to me. I couldn't explain how I solved the problem; I just knew the answer.

One time Tim Allen directed one of the episodes of *Home Improvement*. Tim is one of the funniest guys I know. He walked into the edit room and said, "Come on, old man, let's get this done." He then asked me "What do you do in here all day?"

I answered, "Mostly try to make you look good, but that's not very easy." We had a good laugh, and then we started editing. Tim really knows comedy, and he knows how to get the best out of the material. I enjoyed working with Tim, and I learned a few more things about comedy from him.

Michel Jacobs once asked me if the take I used was the best take on a certain line. I told him I thought it was, but I'd be glad to play all the takes for him. It was very easy to do with Avid. We watched the scene using each different take. Finally Michael said, "That's the one. Put it in." He asked me why I hadn't put that take in from the start, but before I could answer, he looked at me and said, "That was the original take you had in, wasn't it?" I just smiled.

Another time Matt, David, and Carmen from Windancer were in the room editing with me, and they started to tell me what change they wanted. Before they finished, I knew what they were going to ask. By the time they finished their explanation, I had the edit completed. They always accused me of being able to read their minds.

Usually the producers just want the best overall show, while the director is apt to pick a take that has the best camera shot or move, as long as the line reading is OK. The worst is the writer; he or she wants you to use the performance when the actor says the line exactly as written, even if the biggest laugh was on another take when the actor went slightly off script. I can say this because my son, Robert Zappia, was a writer on *Home Improvement*. By the way, one of my proudest moments came when our credits were on the screen on the same show.

Anyway, one of the episodes Robert wrote was three minutes too long. Now, because of the laugh spread during the audience taping and the pacing of the show, you could never know how long a show would end up. I called Robert in the writers' room to ask him if he could come down to the edit bay for a minute. When he arrived, I told him that his episode was three minutes too long. I thought we could lift one whole scene from the show and, even though it was a very funny scene, it wouldn't be missed. I suggested he could use it in another episode. He answered, "You can't do that, Dad! I worked a couple of days writing that scene, and I love it!" Writers—you gotta love them.

I did another show for Matt Williams called *Soul Man* starring Dan Akroyd. The show was shot in New York, so they had to send the tapes to us overnight after the shoot. Then I cut the show on the Disney lot. When it was time for the producers to view the cut and give me notes, we co-ordinated a time with them and booked the satellite feed.

While I was on speakerphone, I played the cut and did the director's notes while he was watching the changes being made on the screen in front of him. Isn't technology great?

No matter how good you are, there's always a chance you may be fired off a project. There are several reasons why this could happen: personality conflicts, political differences, the executives don't feel you're right for the project and, on that rare occasion, something you're doing or not doing, (we all know that could never happen).

I got taken off a project, (OK, fired off a project) three times in my career. In 1989 was the first time involved the *Roseanne* show. Matt Williams, the creator of the show, hired me as the editor the first season, and we really worked well together. About the middle of the second season, Roseanne and Matt couldn't agree on which direction to take her character, so Matt left the show.

The network hired a new show runner, Jeff Harris, who asked me to stay on. The second season director was John Pasquin, who brought his own assistant director. Up to that point I had never worked with either one of them. I was told that the AD didn't like the fact that I was a member of the Directors Guild, which meant I could edit the show and implement director notes without her being in the edit bay with me. At that time editors were finally being considered part of the creative team, so most shows had their editors join the Directors Guild. The AD on *Roseanne* wanted the editing to be done on the studio lot where the show was being shot, but I was working at Compact Video. I guess she just wanted more control of the editing.

After I did the first cut, I sent it to the director. I knew that he'd watch it with the assistant director and give notes, which she would pass on to me. On the fourth episode I sent the cut to the ad for the director's notes. After a couple of days I called the AD to see if she had any notes for me, and she said, "The director hasn't viewed the show yet." I called again a few days later; she said he still hadn't seen the cut. This went on for several episodes until finally the producer called and said that they wanted to move the show to another facility on the CBS Radford lot, and they would also provide their own editor.

I told the producer I understood and I'd have all of the material ready for them, including the edit list of the episode I was working on, and if the editor had any problems or questions he could call me at any time. Every day I would call to tell them that everything was ready to be picked up. After about ten days, I called to tell them that they had to pick up the material immediately because it was all stacked in my editing room. Finally they picked up the show material, and I found out what was really going on.

The *Roseanne* director, John Pasquin, had been steadily and promptly giving the AD his notes on the show during all those times she told me he wasn't even viewing the cuts. Moreover, she had been telling him that she passed along his notes to me, but that I said I would do them when I had the time. You can imagine how this went over with the director.

So for weeks it looked like I had the notes and wouldn't do them, when in fact she had the notes and wouldn't give them to me. In addition, after they decided to take the show to the studio to edit, she told them that I wouldn't release the tapes. At that time I was editing five different shows, so if she had just come to me and said that the producers wanted the show edited at the studio, I would've been glad to turn the show over to them.

As time went on, the AD started directing and, for the first and only time in my career, whenever a client wanted me to edit a show I would say, "I'd be glad to, but only if so-and-so is not directing." When they asked me why, I would just say, "It's a personal thing, but I'm sure she's a very good director, and a lot of good editors will work with her."

A year or so later, Gayle Maffeo called and said that Matt Williams wanted me to edit *Home Improvement*. When she told me that John Pasquin was directing, I asked, "Does he really want to work with me after what happened on the *Roseanne* show?" Gayle replied, "I told him that you would never do anything like that, and that he should at least work with you on the pilot."

The first day of editing was a little tense. However, as time went on, John and I worked together like we'd known each other for years. After that I worked with John for a couple of seasons on *Home Improvement*. On every project John did after that, he would call me to see if I was available to edit for him.

The second time I got fired was in 2001 which concerned the Bette Midler sitcom. It was a show about Bette Midler playing Bette Midler. Great casting, right? That's what I thought, but when I used the funniest takes of Bette playing Bette, the producers said that those takes were "too big." I told them that I used the takes because the audience loved them, and if they didn't want her to act like Bette Midler, why did they have her play herself? Well, I guess they didn't appreciate it.

One week they called me at home and said that I had been replaced because I didn't understand the concept of the show. I guess they were right because I always thought that a sitcom should be funny. Also, when you have a star like Bette Midler, who is one of the greatest talents around whether it's music, comedy, or drama, you let her take the script and run with it. Ninety-nine percent of the time you'll get the results you and the audience want. Two weeks later I was sorry to hear that the show was cancelled.

The third time I got the boot was in 2002 on a show called *My Wife And Kids*. I started editing the show during the second season. The executive producer, Don Reo, and I got along great. The show had different directors every week who very seldom came to editing, so after I finished my first cut, Don and the star of the show, Damon Wayans, viewed the cut with me and gave their notes. At the end of the season, the associate producer called me into his office and said that Damon wanted to hire a friend of his to edit the show, and they wouldn't need me anymore. He said that Don wanted me to stay, but Damon wanted the change.

The last show I did before I semi-retired was *8 Simple Rules to Dating My Teenage Daughter*. The director was Jamie Widdoes, one of the easiest directors to work with. He was not only a nice guy but also a very good director. He shot the show in a way that made it very easy to cut together.

From an editor's point of view, I think a good director is one who knows how to get the right performances out of the actors. He should know how to use the cameras to tell the story, and he has to be able to deal with all personalities.

When I edited *8 Simple Rules*, I worked mostly with one of the producers, Floyd Suarez. Our instincts were very much alike. After I did Jamie's notes, Floyd would come down to my edit bay and, as we watched the show, he gave me the producers' notes. Once the producers' notes were done, I called Floyd back to view what I had done. He would always say, "OK, I'm here to fix your work. Let's play the show and see what you've screwed up."

During my thirty-five years of editing, I don't think I've ever gone on the set of any show except for a pilot or two. I was always editing too many shows at once, and I didn't have the time. However, *8 Simple Rules* was the only show I was doing then, so I finally had time. I went on the set for the taping of this show, and the atmosphere was amazing. John Ritter made you feel as if you were attending a party every Friday night. In between takes he had the people in the audience laughing so hard they couldn't stop. It took a while to settle everybody down so we could continue to tape. John was great with the crew and everybody on the set. He just wanted to show everyone how happy he was that they came to see him.

At the end of the first season, as was the custom, a cast and crew picture was scheduled. I had lost track of time and was absent. John asked someone where I was, then said, "Go get Marco, and we'll wait." In forty years of editing, the cast and crew picture of *8 Simple Rules* is the only one in which I participated

SEASON ONE
2002-2003

In the last episode we did with John, he had as a guest one of his very good friends, Henry Winkler. They were great together. I went home on a Wednesday night ready to come back in the next day to edit a couple of scenes that were pre-shot and were to be played to the audience at the audience taping. Around 10:00 p.m. I got a call from Judy Raugh, the associate producer. She asked if I was sitting down, and I said, "Sure, what's up?"

Judy said, "John Ritter just passed away at St. Joseph's hospital."

I was completely shocked. I felt as if I had lost a close family member. I asked, "How? What happened?" Judy said, "He wasn't feeling very well this evening, so they decided to take him to St. Joseph's emergency room just to be safe. But he just got worse, and his heart finally gave out."

The next day we all went in: Katy Segal and the rest of the cast, the crew, the producers, and some ABC people. We were still trying to figure out what had happened. The set had been so alive when John was there. We were expecting him to walk in at any time and say, "Gotcha!" Everyone who had something to say about John got up and spoke. The whole morning was very moving and surreal. ABC was trying to decide whether to continue the show without John or just end it.

The network decided to end the season with a two-part episode that told how John's character got killed in an auto accident. I've got to tell you these were the two toughest episodes I had ever edited in my thirty-five years as an editor. The episodes dealt with John's passing, the family grieving, and the funeral arrangements. When the script called for the cast to cry, there wasn't any acting on stage that night; those were real tears, and it was very hard for the cast members to hold themselves together. After the taping of each scene, they had to regain their composure to continue.

John was a real gentleman and a hellava nice guy. It was a privilege to have worked with him. The show went on for one more season, but it just didn't work without John. After the show ended, I semi-retired, partially because of John's death and partially because I thought it was time.

I could not help thinking back to when we had viewings with the producers in the edit room. When I finished the first cut, I viewed it a couple times and I thought to myself, "It's perfect I can't imagine what they'd want to change."

Then the Director and Producer's came in to view my perfect cut. During these viewings I always felt like I was back in school and being graded on my homework.

I started the viewing and I would watch them and every once in a while they would write something down on their note pads. I thought to myself, "What notes could they possibly give me it was perfect."

After the viewing was over they gave me their notes. I couldn't believe I was given notes. When I got a performance note I would ask them "what are you looking for in a performance. I knew that when looking at performances it could be very subjective.

After they left the room I started working on their changes, I was amazed to see how much these notes improved the show. When I couldn't give them exactly what they wanted, I'd fine a way to do a cut that would accomplish the same thing.

That's when I realized that during the process of doing the notes I was learning a great deal from these talented people.

From then on I looked forward to these viewing and I was anxious to see what more I could learn.

I started in the industry in 1968 when the only way you could edit for television was to cut two-inch videotape with a razor blade. I have worked with every editing technology since then. Today you can cut a film on a laptop computer at home using digital technology.

A good editor must have a delicate balance between technical know-how, inventiveness, creative ability, and social grace.

Just remember one thing: if you think you're the smartest guy in the room, keep it to yourself and **"Check Your Ego at the Door!"** There will always be somebody in the room from whom you can learn something.

Printed in Great Britain
by Amazon

57221932R00106